SUSTAINIST
DESIGN
GUIDE

T0271552

SUSTAINIST DESIGN GUIDE

How sharing, localism, connectedness and proportionality are creating a new agenda for social design

Michiel Schwarz
Diana Krabbendam
WITH THE BEACH NETWORK

BISPUBLISHERS

4

Content

Preface:
a guide of exploration

This book charts a future that we already inhabit. It connects a vision of a changing culture to what's already happening today in the "design" of a better world. Although there is much talk about a crisis, we feel the future is bright. When we go back to its roots, the word "crisis" means "turning point." It offers an opportunity to transition into a fundamentally new stage.

Cultural boundaries are shifting. There's an enormous wave of new social initiatives worldwide, where millions of dedicated people are beginning to "design" a different kind of environment for themselves that is more collaborative, more socially just, and more sustainable. This movement is what the Sustainist Design Guide is all about.

We build on the perspective of "sustainism"—a concept that one of us, Michiel Schwarz (in collaboration with Joost Elffers), has advanced to mark the new ethos of our day and age. Sustainism represents a shift not only in thinking and doing but in the collective perception of how we live, do business, feed ourselves, build our communities and communicate, as much as how we deal with nature.

The cultural movement that we're seeing offers opportunities for lasting social change, but until now a comprehensive framework has been lacking. We need new ways of looking and of doing in order to play a meaningful part in it. The need for relevant perspectives is what has inspired us to compile this Sustainist Design Guide. The promise is considerable: design can be a tool for social change. And we think it should be. It is no longer a matter of designing for society, but within it.

There is a sense of urgency as well as opportunity. Whilst a global movement is picking up speed, many of us are searching for ways to make meaningful contributions. Creating social value is increasingly becoming a strong incentive for designers as the cultural transformation we are witnessing is emphasising the importance of their role. Meanwhile, the very word "designer" is taking a new shape. Essentially, everyone is now a designer in his or her own right, as people are increasingly able to take their lives in their own hands and redesign their own brand of society.

A CALL FOR ACTION

What we have produced is no ordinary guide. It is an exploration that ventures into new territory, mapping the new domain of design thinking and practice that we have called "sustainist design." This new territory cannot be wholly understood if we apply terminology to it that originated in the previous era. A new language is needed in order to grasp what is happening and how we can make a difference. We have used case studies to try to load our new language with meaning. Each of these case studies holds a promise. Each of them teaches us important lessons, but they also have collective symbolic value. Their global scope tells us that we are now talking about a worldwide movement.

In that sense, this guide is a call to action. Ultimately, by making this book, we intend to shift the design agenda a little. But first and foremost, we hope to shift the discourse of the design agenda. We wish to extend an open invitation to jointly explore the social role of design and designers in shaping our joint future. We have laid down some markers, but the real start is now. We hope our guide will encourage a fruitful dialogue, regardless of its precise content. It should represent a design approach within society: it is a design challenge in itself.

COLLABORATIVE EFFORT

This book grew out of our combined interest in connecting the ideas of sustainist culture to real-life initiatives and opportunities in "social design." Embracing an open source approach, we opened up the research process through an online platform (opensustainistdesign.net) and invited others to contribute social design stories. Both the web platform and this Sustainist Design Guide were developed in close partnership with a small editorial team from the Amsterdam-based The Beach network, including Bas Ruyssenaars, Mira de Graaf, Steffie Verstappen, and designer Robin Uleman. Their contributions, along with those that were made on our web platform, represent a significant part of our collaborative effort.

Now that the guide is out here, it's up to you, and all of us, to further explore how the concept of sustainist design might lead us to a daily practice that is both socially and ecologically sustainable.

Michiel Schwarz and Diana Krabbendam
Amsterdam, April 2013

SUSTAINIST DESIGN

—

What does it mean?

→ EVE BLOSSOM,
*Material Change: Design
Thinking and the Social
Entrepreneurship
Movement*, 2011

66**There is something going on in design— something powerful. People have realised a simple truth: design is a legitimate way to change the world** 99

SOCIAL DESIGN IN THE ERA OF SUSTAINISM

The changing face of design: the designer as **social innovator**

Design for social innovation is on the rise. Design was never divorced from its social uses and impacts, but it is now moving into a fundamentally new stage. After a long period in which design was predominantly focused on functionality, form and aesthetics, we now witness a growing interest in applying design to creating social value. Over the last decade, designers have turned their attention increasingly towards social issues —from healthcare and food to neighbourhood services and community building. As a result, the agenda for design has broadened well beyond traditional functional products and services to include social needs and citizens' concerns.

Under the banner of "social design" new practices have emerged where designers are applying their skills and methods to advance social change. Social good is becoming a key driver for design and designers in many domains of society. The growing use of the very term "social design" can be seen as a sign that what designers are expected to do and make is changing. More significant still, the rise of social design signifies a shift in the role that designers are playing—and perhaps should play—in society. As social needs and social values are increasingly brought into design, the design agenda is taking on a more explicit ethical dimension.

Social design, or "design for social impact" as it is sometimes called, has taken designers into a new territory. The movement towards a greater social role of designers adds an extra layer to the broadening professional design field that has been evolving for decades. Today, the scope of design practice ranges from the design of products and architecture to service design, media design, experience design, and the design of situations. In all of these fields, we have seen a recent turn towards design for social impact and social needs.

At the same time, we see a growing interest from the public and private sectors, and society at large, to turn to designers for answers to questions that previously were the exclusive domain of corporate innovation and public policy. In this context, a new area of design practice has emerged, commonly referred to as "design thinking": the application of design approaches, methods and tools to resolving social and business issues. As IDEO design thinking pioneers Tim Brown and Jocelyn Wyatt explain: "Design thinking addresses the needs of the people who will consume a product or service and the infrastructure that enables it. Non-profits are beginning to use design thinking to develop better solutions to social problems."

Socially responsible design

The changing landscape of design is marked by a focus on its social dimensions. With it comes a turn not only towards the social values to which design is put, but also towards a growing sense of responsibility. In recent years, notions such as "corporate social responsibility" or "socially and ethically responsible consumption" have become accepted phrases. As the social role of design is changing, we may ask: what does it mean to be "responsible" designers? Phrased in such terms, the rise in social design could herald a shift in our attitude towards design, not only by looking for ways of applying design to advancing the social good, but also by asking what it means to be a "designer" in the 21st century.

The rise of the designer as social innovator raises questions about how the practice of design must change to live up to its new role. Equally, if social design is about applying design to creating social value, we need to open up the debate on the social agenda for design. As is the case in any exploration, we need to map the terrain in which we wish to journey in order to explore such questions. In other words, before we can chart a future for social design we have to look at the broader landscape in which we find ourselves at the outset.

Sustainability beyond "green"

We view the growing social role of designers as part of the broader shift that is taking place within society. The world of design is changing, but so is the world itself. As economic models are being fundamentally questioned, old institutions break down, and social values are changing, there is much talk about a "transition" into a new era.

One major social transition that defines the current era is a growing awareness of the environmental impacts of our actions. But we would be missing the point if we would view the movement towards sustainability in terms of ecological issues alone. Today, sustainability has everything to do with how we live and how we wish to shape our living environments. Ecological concerns have become part of a wider agenda of change, socially, economically, and—as this design guide sets out to expose —culturally, too.

Hence, sustainability is much more than "green." The sustainability agenda has as much to do with social concerns and lifestyles, as it does with ecological issues. The growth of the Transition Network movement is a case in point. Worldwide, there are now more than 1,000 "transition towns." They aim at creating not only eco-towns and eco-cities, but at the same time altogether different social environments that are more community-oriented, healthy, and creative. Transition towns are as much about lifestyles as they are about the environment, about liveability as much as climate change. The initiators of one of Europe's leading transition towns, Bristol Green Capital, sum up their mission as follows: "We pledge to make Bristol a low carbon city with a high quality of life for all." Here and elsewhere, sustainability and social innovation are inexorably linked. "Eco" and "socio" need to be addressed together. This reality is defining the new context of social design.

The **largest movement** the world has ever seen

Over the last several years, we are experiencing a shift towards ecological lifestyles and social initiatives, that can be seen in a wide range of developments —whether we look at new attitudes to food and the rise of farmers markets, and cooperatives, local currencies, or the revival of do-it-yourself. At the same time, we see collaboration, open source and co-creation gaining ground in many fields of innovation, often made possible by new social media networks. Equally, we are witnessing a resurgence of small-scale, hands-on, and local approaches to social issues. Collectively, such trends represent a significant transition in the way we experience everyday life, and is essentially a transition to new modes of living with new values and attitudes.

Locally as well as globally we see a new mentality arising where "sustainable living" is becoming shorthand for both social and cultural values. It is fuelled by a growing awareness of the fact that social innovation and sustainable strategies are part of the same agenda. At a minimum, they are two sides of the same coin.

Over the last decades, a worldwide surge of initiatives has rallied around such a social-sustainable agenda, focusing on healthier, socially just, and ecological modes of living. According to American environmentalist and entrepreneur Paul Hawken, there are already over 200 million people worldwide—part of the one million-plus grassroots organisations —who are actively engaged in sustainable ways of living. It is a veritable sustainability and social justice movement that Hawken qualifies as "the largest movement the world has ever seen."

A **cultural shift**: a change in collective outlook

The worldwide movement towards more ecologically and socially responsible lifestyles amounts to a cultural movement. A movement that is growing globally and locally. It reflects a transition in culture. And by "culture" we mean the ideas and values we live by as well as our collective perceptions. What we see happening—and what has provided the impetus for developing this *Sustainist Design Guide*—is that the most significant transition comes from a changing outlook on what we value and how we wish to shape our life-world. It can rightly be called a "paradigm shift," or a transition from one coherent set of cultural values, ideas, and principles to another.

A new way of living is emerging in which, as web editor Beth Buczynski has paraphrased it, "access is valued over ownership, experience is valued over material possessions, and 'mine' becomes 'ours' so everyone's needs are met without waste." Such expressions reflect a change in our social mindset and in the ways we wish to design our living environments. They herald a change in *zeitgeist*.

The **playing field** is changing

This shift in culture is both a challenge and an opportunity—both for designers and "non-designers." As the playing field is changing, questions are raised about the social role of the (professional) designer. It is important to gain insight into what it means when the citizen, the city dweller, the client and the user become the new players in a process of "co-design." How will the new context change the nature of the design process and what does this imply for our eventual designs? Equally, if social good and sustainability are becoming key drivers for innovation, where do different practices of design fit in? Who are the players as the playing field evolves? And what will be the rules of the game?

The cultural transitions in society, and the new arena they are creating, prompt us to re-examine the meaning of social design. In the past, the social dimensions of design were often framed as a question of assessing social impacts at the very end of the design process. But today's growing concern for "design for social impact" is driven by a different agenda. It puts the social dimension upfront and emphasises the needs and social good that the design is to serve. It amounts to a recasting of social design. In the new playing field, we need design approaches that are sensitive to the changing culture and that can build on the numerous social initiatives that are unfolding around us. That's why we showcase real-life designs that are already doing exactly that (see Part B).

The **new culture** in perspective: "sustainism" as vista point

When we venture into new territory, we are often at a loss to make sense of what we are seeing. How do we navigate a new landscape, a city we have not visited before, or a culture that is foreign to us? We try and get some sense of place and direction, some kind of overview of where we are, and where we could be heading. This holds true for the new cultural landscape in which we find ourselves today. Of course we cannot step outside of our own culture, but what we can do is to look for a perspective—a vista point if you wish—from which to bring our newly emerging culture into view. Only then can we begin to chart our paths in the new territory.

A first step is to appreciate the fact that culture, and design culture, is indeed changing. But how to interpret what is happening? The new culture we talk about is already here. Until now we have given a hazy picture of what it looks like. Yet, with examples of transition towns, urban farming, cradle-to-cradle design, ethical consumption and socially responsible business—to flag just a few—it does not take much to see that attitudes are shifting in a very grand way. It is happening in many domains, from neighbourhood planning to health and from energy networks to education. Something very fundamental is changing about the way in which we perceive place, time, nature, food, responsibility, consumption, and so on.

Until recently, this change in culture did not have a name. In this guide, we embrace the idea of "sustainism" to name the new culture. The concept of sustainism was first introduced by Michiel Schwarz (one of the authors of this *Sustainist Design Guide*) and Joost Elffers in their 2010 manifesto *Sustainism is the New Modernism*. Sustainism captures a new cultural era and a worldwide movement. It offers a way to bring our changing culture into perspective. Hence, the term "sustainist" as the operative word in the title of this guide. The core idea of sustainism is that we are transitioning to new ways of seeing and doing, which is creating a collective culture that is more connected, more localist, and more ecologically and socially sustainable. [See page 019 *Sustainism manifesto*]. Sustainism provides us with a cultural map of the where we find ourselves and where we may be going.

This guide is inspired by the idea that the perspective of sustainism not only captures some essential features of what is going on culturally, but that it can also provide us with a rewarding framework for how to look at design and innovation that is both socially and ecologically sustainable. We view the sustainist perspective as an insightful "lens" to explore how social design practice is changing and what this implies for the design agenda of the future.

Towards a **new agenda** for social design: sightlines & guidelines

In this guide, we set out to develop the sustainist perspective as a framework for a new social and sustainable design agenda. Sustainism is as much a way of seeing and doing, as it is a new era and a movement. In a front page strapline the *International Herald Tribune* called sustainism "a new ethos for design." The word "ethos" strikes at the heart of the cultural shift towards sustainism. It implies both a set of fundamental values and an action perspective.

With this guide, we wish to open the debate about what the new sustainist ethos could mean for the design agenda. What does it imply for those involved in different forms of social design, both designers and non-designers? How can we begin to develop design thinking and design practice in a sustainist mode? In the era of co-creation and co-design, we deliberately frame this debate as an open question: the answer lies less in defining its exact boundaries and more in what we wish "sustainist design" and its effects to be. The first step in this direction is to expose what a sustainist perspective on social design looks like.

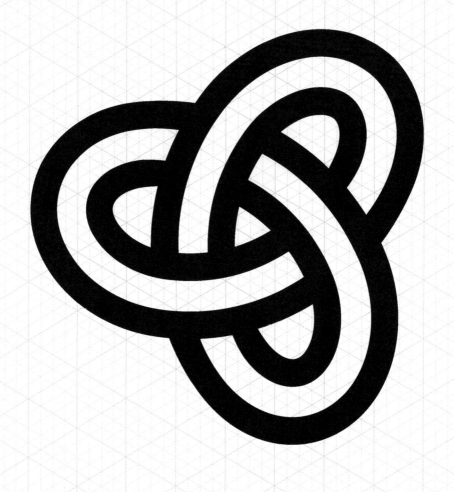

The Trefoil Knot, the symbol of sustainist design represents the idea that in Sustainism everything is interconnected and interdependent. It is one of a series of sustainist symbols designed by JOOST ELFFERS as part of a visual vocabulary for the sustainist era, as published in Sustainism is the New Modernism by MICHIEL SCHWARZ & JOOST ELFFERS.

Like all the visual symbols in the Sustainism manifesto, it may be freely distributed and used non-commercially (with credit to the authors) under a Creative Commons license (by-nc-nd 3.0).

"Sustainism"—a concept coined by Michiel Schwarz and Joost Elffers—names the new context of global connectivity, sustainability, open exchange, and a resurgence of the local. Sustainism builds on the changing focus and attitude that marks 21st century mainstream culture. The international press has called sustainism **"a new ethos for design."** In the view of Schwarz and Elffers, it will become the leading force in design and innovation, as we collectively discover what meanings we wish to give to sustainist culture.

The concept of sustainism was introduced by Schwarz and Elffers in their graphic Sustainism manifesto.* Under the rubric of sustainism, they chart a culture that is more **connected**, more **localised**, and more **sustainable**. The culture of sustainism builds on the 200+ million-people "sustainability movement," but is also the culture of **sharing**, social media, "Generation We," and new forms of localism. In the words of the authors, **sustainist culture** has emerged as "the confluence of globalisation, the web, climate change, localism, media democracy, open source, environmentalism, and more," and it is built on "a collective worldview that stresses the interdependence among cultural and natural environments."

Sustainism heralds a new cultural era, as we transition **from modernity to sustainity**. It invites new types of design, architecture and social innovation, conceived out of an inte-grated perspective that has as much to do with the networked world and connecting people as it has with ecology and sustainability.

*Sustainism is the New Modernism: A Cultural Manifesto for the Sustainist Era, MICHIEL SCHWARZ & JOOST ELFFERS, 2010, D.A.P./Distributed Art Publishers New York.

→ GEOFF MULGAN,
Saffron Woodcraft et al.,
Design for Social Sus-
tainability: A framework
for creating thriving new
communities, 2011

"The great challenge of twenty-first century design is mastering ecological and social design"

LOOKING AT DESIGN THROUGH A SUSTAINIST LENS

SUSTAINABLE INNOVATION
×
SOCIAL DESIGN
=
SUSTAINIST DESIGN

Sustainism as lens:
shifting our perspective on social design

Sustainism, or whatever we wish to call the current cultural movement, provides us with a perspective through which to look at problems. Equally, it will shape what we perceive to be solutions to those problems. Such is the power of culture: we share a collective view of the world and we organise and design our lives accordingly. The idea of sustainist culture not only captures the current *zeitgeist*, it also provides us with a lens through which to (re)view design for social impact and sustainable life.

A sustainist take on the social design agenda literally begins with a shift in perspective, a different way of looking at the world. That's what those calling sustainism the "new ethos for design" refer to. It captures a way of seeing, a perception of the world, and what we value. But when paradigms change, there is much more going on than a shift in collective perception. The transition to sustainist culture consists not just of what we "see" and value (*ethos*), it also involves what we "think" (*eidos*) and "do" (*praxis*).

A sustainist stance on design, therefore, is more than just a point of view: it is also a mentality and a way of doing. That is what we wish to bring into perspective when we look at the agenda and practice of social design.

ETHOS-EIDOS-PRAXIS

Understanding the sustainist paradigm shift in terms of ethos-eidos-praxis leads us to raise three kinds of questions in relation to our exploration of sustainist design:

HOW DO WE ENVISION AND VALUE SOCIAL AND SUSTAINABLE DESIGN?

WHAT ARE THE RELEVANT GUIDING CONCEPTS THAT ARE ADVANCING SUSTAINABLE AND SOCIAL DESIGN?

AND, WHAT PRACTICES ARE EMERGING IN SUSTAINIST DESIGN?

Together as well as separately they point us towards a road map to review the agenda for social and sustainable design in the sustainist era.

Sustainist **style**

Sustainism implies a new outlook on how we shape our living environments and a new set of fundamental ideas that informs what we see as feasible, desirable, and valuable. In the domain of design—among many other social domains—we are seeing a transition from one cultural paradigm to another. Following Schwarz and Elffers, we frame this shift by contrasting modernist with sustainist ways of organising and shaping our living environments. The title of their cultural manifesto, *Sustainism is the New Modernism*, expresses this.

By renaming "what is going on," we try to bring into focus how the practice of design and design thinking is shifting: from modernist foundations towards sustainist principles. We can make this shift tangible by contrasting the "modernist style" with a—yes, still emerging—"sustainist style." Whereas modernist culture embraced the linear, the centralised, the machine, and the uniform, sustainist culture by contrast favours the cyclical, the network, nature, and diversity. Once we list some of the defining features of a sustainist style (as we do in the Box below: *Modernist versus Sustainist Style*), we will begin to see how it shifts design (and more) towards an inherently different development path than the familiar 20th century modernist one.

MODERNIST VERSUS SUSTAINIST STYLE	
MODERNIST	SUSTAINIST
LESS IS MORE	DO MORE WITH LESS
OBJECTS	CONNECTIONS
CENTRALISED	NETWORKED
STAND-ALONE DESIGNS	SYSTEM DESIGNS
AUTONOMOUS	INTERDEPENDENT
FORM FOLLOWS FUNCTION	FORM FOLLOWS MEANING
PLANNING	CODESIGN
LINEAR	CYCLICAL
UNIVERSAL	CONTEXT-SPECIFIC
CLOSED	OPEN
EFFICIENT	EFFECTIVE
DISPOSABLE	CRADLE-TO-CRADLE
CONTROLLING NATURE	WORKING WITH NATURE
UNIFORM	DIVERSIFIED
GLOBALISED	PLACE-BASED
NATURE AS RESOURCE	NATURE AS SOURCE

Based on *Sustainism is the New Modernism: A Cultural Manifesto for the Sustainist Era*, MICHIEL SCHWARZ & JOOST ELFFERS, 2010, D.A.P./Distributed Art Publishers New York.

Sustainist **design**: what do we mean?

We have been speaking about "sustainist design," but what exactly do we mean? Can we tell you what it is? Yes and no. Sustainism offers us a vantage point and context for seeing how social design is shifting its focus towards a particular set of social issues and sustainability concerns. At the same time, we raise it as an open question deliberately. What sustainist design is, and can turn into, is something we have to find out together.

In fact, the desire to make this question explicit and share and discuss it with designers and non-designers is what has driven this *Sustainist Design Guide*. We have called it a guide in the sense that we aim to explore different paths and crossroads in the new territory where design for social innovation and sustainability meet. We view it as a first exploratory "travel guide" for the emerging practice of what we have termed sustainist design.

We do not start our exploration empty-handed. The sustainist perspective gives us a number of meaningful starting points. The shape of what the new sustainist culture implies for design is already somewhat visible. One way to define sustainist design is to categorise it as design that connects social and ecological sustainability. To address an oft-asked important question: sustainist design goes well beyond "green." Although it may include eco-design, sustainist design is just as much concerned with connectedness, local values, and community as drivers of social innovation.

One defining feature of sustainist design then is that it forges a fundamental connection between "design for sustainability" and "design for social impact." The domain of sustainist design sits at the crossover between sustainable and social design. In other words: *sustainable innovation x social design = sustainist design*. This offers us a starting point from which to start exploring.

SUSTAINIST DESIGN

SUSTAINABLE INNOVATION

×

SOCIAL DESIGN

=

SUSTAINIST DESIGN

The value of **values in design**

Design has always evolved with the times and is inherently adaptive. Designers are particularly responsive to the demands of their customers— be they consumers, industrial users, or public organisations. As technologies change, production techniques advance, and consumption patterns shift, designers come up with new products and services. But now, in the early 21st century, we observe fundamental changes in consumer and end users' expectations. They expect design to deliver more than functional and aesthetic answers to problems. Increasingly, a new social agenda is emerging, driven by the question of what values and purpose are served by design. That's where design for social innovation and sustainability fits in. And where the rise in design thinking stems from.

The social and ethical turn in design is essentially a shift towards a human-centred and value-driven design process. Over the last decades we have seen an increasing focus on innovation and design that is geared towards creating social value. This is part of a significant shift that is materialising in our approaches to design: from function to meaning. It also defines the growing attention for creativity and "creative innovation" (as The Beach network, one of the initiators of this guide has termed it).

Moreover, shifting values are also driving a change in lifestyles. Look at the recent trend towards a new set of "valued resources," social as well as economic: attributes such as creativity, time, information, and community. Such values are forging a new way of living, which the American sociologist Juliet Schor has called a "plenitude lifestyle." Connected to such valued attributes, millions of people are embracing "caring for the planet" as an important value to aspire to. That's why it comes as no surprise that, in the domain of social innovation and sustainability, we see a revival of attention for social values.

Four sustainist **design qualities**

The central idea of this guide is to explore how a number of core values that are emerging in "sustainist life" can inform the design agenda of the future. In the era of sustainism, we are moving towards an altogether different set of design qualities than the one we used in the past. We are not alone in this observation. Design thinker Ezio Manzini for example has drafted an agenda for social innovation and sustainability leading to designs that are "small, local, open and connected."

The design field is shifting in many ways. We witness a trend towards greater inclusiveness, openness, and community in design processes. The open source movement and the trend of collaborative design are the most visible. Under the header of sustainist design, we could group the numerous innovations that involve some form of co-design: design with people, with communities, and with nature. And the question of how design can be used to create social value is becoming increasingly relevant among designers. The concept of "added value" used to refer to economics and economic yield. Today, it is increasingly concerned with social and cultural values instead.

Clearly, when we speak of such sweeping changes in our culture, there are many ways to interpret the new mindset and practice of sustainist life. In an attempt to tease out some underlying drivers of change, we are focusing on a set of four defining qualities that we believe span the new arena of sustainist design: sharing, localism, connectedness and proportionality. They are concerned, respectively, with the value of collaboration, the growing value of networked relationships, a rediscovered sense of place, and the appreciation of human dimensions. In the *Sustainism manifesto*, these sustainist qualities are captured in four aphorisms. In this guide, we turn them to social and sustainable design.

SUSTAINISM MANIFESTO APHORISMS

WE ARE WHAT WE SHARE

LOCAL IS A QUALITY, NOT A GEOGRAPHICAL MARKER

IT'S ALL ABOUT RELATIONSHIPS

PROPORTIONALITY RATHER THAN SCALE

Sharing, localism, connectedness, and proportionality. These four design qualities are not exclusive, neither do they limit the kind of attributes that are relevant for the further development of sustainist design and sustainist design practice. As is the case with any exploration into a new terrain, there are different paths that one can travel. What these sustainist qualities chart—separately and together—are the kind of qualitative attributes that we envision to be of importance for the future of social design. We believe that these qualities capture some of the fundamental value shifts that will drive the emerging social design agenda. They provide us with parameters for making sense of recent social design initiatives. And they pinpoint the rough outline of the debate on the social relevance of design.

Sustainist **design briefs**

As said before, a sustainist perspective on design makes both social design and eco-design part of a new cultural agenda. If social good and sustainability are becoming drivers for innovation, these four qualities can open up the conceptual space for sustainist design. The central question that we wish to raise in this publication is how these and other sustainist attributes may be designed into products, services, experiences, and social situations.

As design thinker Tim Brown reminds us, the classic starting point of many a design project is its brief: "a set of mental constraints that gives the design team a framework from which to begin." The sustainist perspective offers us such a framework. It challenges us to bring the new sustainist values into our design briefs, as starting points rather than outcomes. The four qualities that we are advancing as key features of sustainist culture will (re)shape the design process and inform the social impact of design.

At the heart of this guide is a shift in focus that challenges us to bring the four sustainist values of sharing, localism, connectedness and proportionality into our design briefs. On the *Open Book for Sustainist Design* website, which functioned as an open online platform for developing this guide, we opened this discussion by posing four design challenges. Taking a leaf out of the how-might-we approach used by the innovative OpenIDEO programme, we asked:

HOW MIGHT WE DESIGN?

HOW MIGHT WE DESIGN FOR SHARING?

HOW MIGHT WE DESIGN FOR LOCALISM?

HOW MIGHT WE DESIGN FOR CONNECTEDNESS?

HOW MIGHT WE DESIGN FOR PROPORTIONALITY?

These four questions then became the prism through which we began to look at the changing field of design for social impact and sustainability. They are mere entry points that help us to see the new shape of the emerging social design agenda.

We invite you to accept these four qualities as an initial outline for recognising sustainist design criteria. They provide us with the "lines of sight" to explore what sustainist design could mean. They are our pathfinders.

→ MICHIEL SCHWARZ
& JOOST ELFFERS
authors of *Sustainism
is the New Modernism*,
2010

"**Sustainism implies new criteria for our design briefs, involving qualities such as sharing, localism, connectedness, and proportionality, as well as environmental sustainability**"

SUSTAINIST DESIGN QUALITIES

Collaboration

Open
exchange

Commons

SHARING

Design for sharing —we are what we share

A new culture of sharing is emerging. We are increasingly sharing goods, places, services and information. It is creating social value and community. In this way, shareability is becoming a valued quality that drives new business practices, community cooperatives, and new forms of "collaborative consumption." The open source movement and the emerging open design practice reflect the same mentality. Centred around collaboration and exchange, sharing schemes are often linked to mobile and Internet technologies.

The sustainist design challenge is as follows: **what would happen if "shareability" would be taken as a design criterion?** How might we bring shareable assets into the design process for products, services, environments and situations? What might we (re)design to encourage more sharing and open exchange?

"Sharing is cool: It's good for business, the community and the planet"

→ RACHEL BOTSMAN,
global thought leader on
collaborative consumption

THE SHARING SOCIETY IS HERE

New sharing-based initiatives in business and social entrepreneurship are being launched everyday. So much so that we can rightly speak of the emergence of a "sharing society" and a "sharing economy." In the sharing society, people share tools, services, knowledge, places, and skills. We have seen the success of car sharing as a prominent example, including local initiatives that enable us to rent our neighbour's car. The sharing economy has grown rapidly. We now see local sharing systems for a wide variety of things, from textbooks to tools and from toys to clothing. Online sharing of knowledge and expertise has been at the forefront of this trend. This is reflected by worldwide online resources such as Wikipedia, but is also increasingly visible at the local level. Community time banks and co-ops, where expertise and skills are pooled, shared and exchanged, are quickly increasing in popularity. Shared places are on the rise, too—from communal gardens and urban farming to "people's supermarkets" and local public spaces that are collectively designed and run. There are many telling examples in shared services, too. Take the success of Couchsurfing—a worldwide community of over five million members in 100,000 cities that connects travellers to locals who meet offline to share cultures, hospitality and adventures. Airbnb—a community market place for the rental of unique spaces—is another good example. Both are causing a revolution in the tourism business.

COLLABORATIVE LIFESTYLES

What lies behind these examples is a surge in initiatives that are explicitly designed to bring sharing, lending, trading, and swapping into our daily lives. We are beginning to create a lifestyle around sharing. Sharing reflects a shift in society towards collaborative practices and lifestyles. We see many sharing schemes that are part of the rise in "collaborative lifestyles." It is not just physical goods that can be shared, swapped, and bartered. People are uniting in a common purpose to share and exchange less tangible assets such as time, space, skills, and money (collaborativeconsumption.com). As Kim Gaskins (content director at Latitude Research) observes: "Sharing represents a fundamental paradigm shift in how people consume: from hyper-consumption to collaborative consumption— a perfect storm driven by connective technologies, economic recession, and raised environmental consciousness" (shareable.net).

SHARING AS QUALITY

Sharing is becoming a valued quality of life. It combines a number of sustainist features, such as collaboration, connectedness, responsible consumption, "commons," open exchange of information, and sustainability concerns. We value sharing, not just for its economic benefits or positive impacts to the environment, but also for what it brings us socially. A change from "Generation Me" to "Generation We" is becoming visible in many walks of life—from car sharing to swapping products, from open source software to social currencies. Sharing implies building communities. Its social and communal qualities are key to the success of sharing. As American entrepreneur Lisa Gansky (author of *The Mesh*) concludes: "Sharing-based businesses generally offer a greater feeling of connection and community." What we are witnessing is a shift in focus from the individual to the collectivity and the corresponding emergence of a culture of collaboration and exchange.

SHAREABLE DESIGN

Shareability depends as much on open exchange and social networks as on the specific feature of what is being shared. That's why shareable design often starts with the design of social connections. As design thinker Ezio Manzini says: "the act of designing for sharing makes otherwise invisible connections visible." Design for sharing implies a different mode of social exchange and how we do things. As collaborative consumption pioneer Rachel Botsman has formulated the design-for-sharing challenge: "designers must re-imagine not just what we consume, but how we consume."

There are no blueprints to design for sharing and the leads to shareable design will be diverse. The impetus comes from different considerations and opportunities. In some cases, limited resources or environmental concerns are leading. In others, the communal and collaborative aspects of it will drive shareable design. Collaborative practices, open exchange, common resources and community are all features that can be built into our designs.

**TO EXPLORE
SHAREABLE.NET**

Shareable.net is an online magazine and community about the culture and economy of sharing. Shareable is a non-profit online platform that focuses on "sharing by design." The shareable.net website explores "how to design life, work and community, so that people can better share resources." It is a hub for information and exchange to accommodate "people and projects bringing a shareable world to life." Shareable.net is an inspiring resource for all kinds of sharing-based initiatives—sharing of products, services, information, and places. The website maps new social developments based on sharing. It tracks what is happening in the emerging sharing economy and "collaborative consumption" and collaborative lifestyles. It invites people to share news about sharing, so that all of us can "learn about how [we] can lead a more shareable life."

**VIEWPOINT
GUIDE TO SHARING: EXCHANGING STUFF, TIME, SKILLS AND SPACE**

"Sharing implies a different approach to ownership of the goods, services, skills, and talents that abound in a community. Through sharing systems, we can get the utility out of goods and services without the burden of ownership—in ways that help build community, clear clutter, and allow for more equitable access to resources. The "access-over-ownership" model frees us from having to make, buy, and consume ever more stuff, saving our pocketbooks and reducing our environmental impact."

→ *Guide to Sharing: Exchanging Stuff, Time, Skills and Space*, The Center for a New American Dream, 2013

Community

Local
experiences

Rootedness

LOCALISM

Design for localism —local is a quality, not a place marker

The local is something we increasingly value. It is no longer just a geographic marker, but has become a quality in and of itself. While the world is more globalised than ever before, we see a simultaneous resurgence of localism: a longing for local qualities and belonging. Localism is the next global trend. The new localism is essentially about giving meaning to local connections, local relations, and local rootedness. New forms of localism, where the local and the global are no longer opposites, are a hallmark of sustainism. In social design, this often implies adopting the well-known social activists' call to "think global, act local."

The sustainist design challenge is as follows: **how might we (re)design our living environments to enhance local qualities and experiences?** How might we design for localist attributes such as sense of place, locally rooted experiences, neighbourhood, and community building? How can we give meaning to the local, whilst acknowledging that all locals are (or can be) globally connected?

"Here is where we meet"

→ JOHN BERGER,
writer and storyteller

EMBRACING A NEW "LOCAL"

The "local" is experiencing a revival. We see a resurgence of localism and a longing for a return to local experiences, local relationships, and a local sense of place. Whilst our lives are more globalised than ever, we see a renewed interest in local qualities. Localism is now a worldwide trend. It is manifested in the increase of local farmers markets (see *To Explore*), the rise of local currencies, the "local food revolution," community-supported farming, and the re-discovered importance of local meeting places.

And whilst we are turning to the local, it is a different kind of local then the one of the past. It's not the old local of the village, where local reality was the only reality, distanced from the rest of world. The growth in local money, locally sourced produce, local energy schemes, and local business development does not mean that those local communities wish to live in isolation. And of course they do not. Today, every place on the globe is now connected 24/7, which is why the global and local are no longer opposites. Many of us are both locally rooted and globally connected. The sustainist world is the world of the local market and Twitter, the corner café and Facebook, the neighbourhood square and CNN. Our designed environments and experiences are a mix between local and global.

NEW FORMS OF LOCALISM IN A GLOBALISED WORLD

In this new context, the nature of "the local" is changing fundamentally. We are searching for new forms of localism, new models based on a sense of place and local relationships, whilst embracing the connected, globalised world that we value, too. The new localism that is emerging often reflects a kind of "glocal" reality. It has local features but is not provincial, unlike the old local. It is a kind of "cosmopolitan local," as design thinker Ezio Manzini has called it. And it is characterised by its diversity: the world can no longer be viewed as a single "global village" (as McLuhan argued in the 1960s), rather, it is a globe of connected villages. What is arising is a kind of localism that has local qualities at its core, but that connects to the global at the same time. Our search for local connections and a new sense of place does not reject global technologies or global connectivity. Instead localist initiatives, especially those in relation to food and energy, clearly connect with global aspirations and concerns—for example, with regard to environmental awareness.

Especially within the urban context, we can see how the local takes on new meanings. Many of us long to be part of local communities and have a local identity, while wanting to be part of global communities at the same time. We have local homes, but also regard the planet as our home. For the first time in human history, people have an actual choice if, when and in what sense they wish to be local—and when they want to be global. We can now be both. This also means that we can design for the specific kind of "local" that we're after.

LOCAL AS VALUE

In sustainist culture, "local" is becoming a value rather than a geographical marker. It is becoming a quality in itself. The local qualities that we value have less to do with a mark on the map, but more with a sense of locality in the relationships we have with place. It is becoming less of an answer to the question "where are you from?" and more about experiencing local relationships, in our neighbourhoods and our physical environments. It entails relationships with the people who make the stuff we buy, the local connections we have with those with whom we share in our communities, as well as our relationship with local nature, local soil, and the land. As the American poet and farmer Wendell Berry eloquently says: "What I stand for is what I stand on."

LOCALIST DESIGN QUALITIES

Local connections, neighbourhood, and community sharing are some of the hallmarks of the new localism that is emerging as a valued quality. The challenge for designers is how to design localist features into their designs. Local farmers markets may point us in the right direction. The way in which they operate may become a conceptual model for designing local economy and local community. It values direct contact between the local producer and consumer and gives us direct knowledge of the specifics of what we buy. What we look for at a farmers market is to be "close to the source," to have a dialogue with the growers and sellers of our food, and to feel part of the regional food culture.

The farmers market model is meaningful, because it is more personal than mass markets, adds "feel good" value, and enhances local community. As environmentalist writer Bill McKibben points out (on the basis of sociological studies), "consumers have ten times as many conversations at farmers markets as they do at supermarkets." The market is a local experience that we can literally relate to. The quality of the local lies in humanising these nearby relationships. The changing outlook on the local can also be seen in planners' call to refocus "from space to place." It is a value shift "from total economy to local economy," to cite Wendell Berry once more. In a similar vein, we need to ask ourselves how we may shift to "local designs." How might we embed local qualities, local identity, and local connections into our designs?

TO EXPLORE
THE FARMERS MARKET & LOCAL COMMUNITY AGRICULTURE

Farmers markets and community supported agriculture initiatives (CSAs) exemplify how the "local" is being re-valued. The rise in local farmers markets is a worldwide phenomenon. Farmers markets and CSAs—in which consumers buy shares of local farm harvests in advance and then routinely reap the benefits in the form of fresh food—have expanded rapidly over the last decade. In the United States, there are currently about 8,000 local farmers markets and their number is growing rapidly by at least 10 new ones per week. Schools, restaurants, supermarkets and other mainstream institutions are buying food from local farmers markets. Most of these markets were independently conceived as local grassroots initiatives.

VIEWPOINT
BUSINESS ALLIANCE FOR LOCAL LIVING ECONOMIES / LOCALISM 101

"To be a localist. Localism is about building communities that are more healthy and sustainable—backed by local economies that are stronger and more resilient. It means we use regional resources to meet our needs—reconnecting eaters with farmers, investors with entrepreneurs, and business owners with the communities and natural places on which they depend. It recognises that not one of us can do it alone and that we're all better off, when we're all better off.

Localists recognise that while our focus is primarily on our own communities, our vision is global. Each of us is crafting a piece of a larger mosaic—a global network of cooperatively interlinked local economies."

→ Localism 101, published on BALLE / Be a Localist, bealocalist.org/Localism-101, 2012

BALLE is a growing North American alliance of nearly 60 fully autonomous local business networks.

Connectivity

Interdependence

Connections

CONNECTEDNESS

Design for connectedness —everything is interconnected

Sustainism is the culture of connectivity and networks: everyone and everything is connected and interdependent. Whether we talk about things, people or environments, it is all about relationships. The metaphor for the new sustainist context is the "web." Connectedness is a core quality in the world of networks, both socially and digitally. To be connected becomes a value in itself. Once we put relationships at the centre of our lives, we are able to recognise how to (re)connect to the natural environment, to our communities, and to the process of making.

The sustainist design challenge is as follows: **what would our world look like if the nature and quality of relationships and connections were at the heart of our designs?** How might connectedness function as a design criterion to help us find design solutions in different contexts? How might we (re)design our living environments and meeting places to encourage building meaningful relationships between people, and within and between communities? And how, within the design process, do we assess the quality of our relationships?

66 The quality of our connections is the key to quality 99

→ RAY & CHARLES EAMES,
twentieth century design pioneers

A CONNECTED WORLD

To say that we live in a connected world is a platitude. Whilst technologies of connectivity have always been important in human communication and social relations, they are now taking on truly global dimensions. The Internet is everywhere. There are six billion mobile phone subscribers. In just one minute, more than 200 million emails are being sent. And Facebook currently connects more than one billion users.

What is significant about the rise of the Internet and the related media networks is not only the sheer numbers and technology, but how it alters the very nature of our relationships. Essentially, the worldwide web is all about connecting to one another, to the goods we buy, and to information. The "connectivity revolution" feeds into the cultural movement of sustainism. As Paul Hawken (author of *Blessed Unrest*) points out: the worldwide social and sustainability movement seeks connection, rather than control.

a living environment where "being connected" is increasingly important in social engagement and connectivity is often at the centre of community.

RELATIONSHIPS AT THE CENTRE

Viewed through a sustainist lens, connectivity is an essential attribute in an increasingly interdependent world where the nature of our relationships will come to define our living environments. But the real operative word is "connectedness" and the ability to make connections, not just to other people but also to our communities, to nature, to information, and to our living environments. Placing connections at the centre of our designs can shift how we view a problem and lead us to different solutions. It also implies a shift in our design perspective: from components that build up the whole to a "systems view" which defines the relevant elements. It makes "building connections" a key focus of design.

THE PRINCIPLE OF "WITH"

The web is an invitation to connect. It represents a mentality of thinking and acting together: with people, rather than for them. That's the cultural power of connectivity and peer networks. As Charles Leadbeater (author of *We-Think*) has it: "If the culture that the web is creating were to be reduced to a single, simple design principle it would be the principle of 'with'. The appeal of the web, however, stems from the way it connects to and amplifies the idea of 'with' in other areas of life."

The collaborative principle of "with" is at the heart of many social innovations. We are creating

CONNECTEDNESS AS VALUE

At the heart of sustainist culture is the idea that everything is interrelated and interdependent. Creating meaningful relationships becomes key. In this sense, connectedness becomes a valued quality and a feature that we can identify and learn to grasp.

The idea of connectedness also implies forging connections in different ways—for example in the way in which we connect with our environment or nature. Or in the way in which we relate to the material world and the products we use. The latter can be seen in the growth of do-it-yourself, the revival of the crafts, and the upcoming "culture of making." By making things, we create connections and engage with the world. Connections essentially build community, as is the case in the Etsy web platform that connects half a million "makers" of handmade goods to over 10 million customers worldwide. Here and elsewhere, "making is connecting," to quote David Gauntlett's book title. Many social innovation projects that involve co-creation reflect a similar quality.

DESIGNING FOR CONNECTEDNESS

Connectedness is a core quality in our networked world. Peer networks are a significant part of designing for connectedness. Building peer networks plays a key role in many community-based forms of social innovation. Steven Johnson, author of *Future Perfect: The Case for Progress in a Networked Age*: "When a need arises in society that goes unmet, our first impulse should be to build a peer network to solve that problem. Some of those networks will relay heavily on digital network technology, as Kickstarter does; others will be built using older tools of community and communications, including that timeless platform of humans gathering in the same room and talking to one another."

Thinking in terms of connections focuses our attention on relationships as a defining feature in design. Designing connections becomes central to creating value. An example of how connecting is the key to creating communities for social design is provided by the OpenIDEO open innovation platform. In one of its design challenges, it highlights the value of creating "connection space" when we design for health care in our local communities. OpenIDEO: "Whether it's in the physical or digital world, the places where we connect with others have a deep impact on the way we treat each other and the environment."

Designing for connectedness thus refocuses our design brief and positions the quality of our relationships at its centre. It is about designing and redesigning relationships that (re)connect us with the natural environment, communities, place, and the land that provides our food. How can the design criterion of connectedness help us find design solutions in the diverse contexts of education, local community, entrepreneurship, creativity, food, the environment, and urban life?

TO EXPLORE
DESIGNING COMMUNITY:
OPENIDEO.COM

OpenIDEO is an open innovation platform, set up to address design challenges for social and environmental impact. OpenIDEO is based on connecting people "collaborating as a global community to tackle some of our world's most pressing issues while pursuing real and positive impact." Since its launch in 2010, OpenIDEO has evolved into a global community of over 40,000 members from 170-plus countries. The concept behind OpenIDEO's design challenges is that ideas emerge best through an open collaborative design process. The platform is maintained by the international design firm IDEO as a way to include non-experts in the design process. Each design challenge moves through three phases: inspiration, concepting, and evaluation. OpenIDEO design challenges that have been developed to date include "How might we enable communities to take more initiative in making their local environments better" and "How might we better connect food production and consumption."

VIEWPOINT
WOODY TASCH / INQUIRIES INTO
THE NATURE OF SLOW MONEY

"There's a need for relationship building. (...) We need to reward those who do not build value on broken relationships, and whose value creation process is built around the preservation and restoration of relationships: relationships between individuals, relationships between producers and consumers and communities, relationships between cultures, relationships between species."

→ Woody Tash, *Inquiries into the Nature of Slow Money: Investing as if food, farms, and fertility mattered*, 2010

43

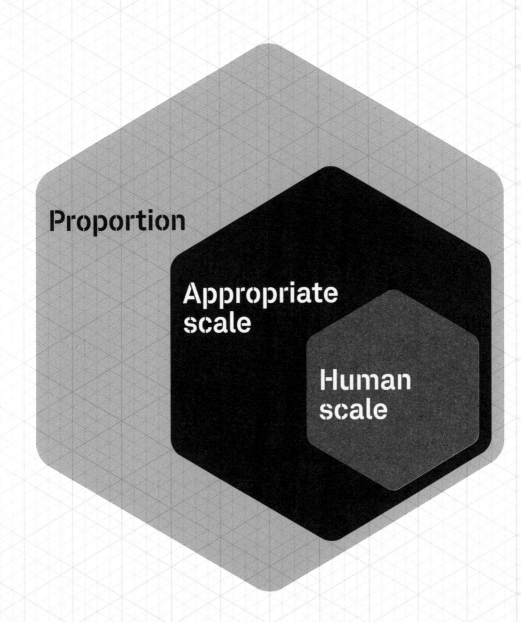

Proportion

Appropriate scale

Human scale

PROPORTIONALITY

Design for proportionality —shifting focus from scale to proportionality

Sustainist approaches to design question the modernist ideas of large-scale and high speed. Bigger and faster is not necessarily better. The idea of proportionality shifts the design agenda towards appropriate size rather than unquestioned upscaling, and towards selective slowness rather than unquestioned speed. Sustainism values the human scale. Sustainist culture encourages us to (re)proportion and relate scale to the social context. It shifts our design focus towards questions of appropriate size and human dimensions: from scale to proportionality.

The sustainist design challenge is as follows: **how might we design for an appropriate scale?** And how can we tell when our designs are out of proportion? What might a design for limited dimensions look like? How might we design for "slow" products, experiences, situations, and environments?

66 There is a human scale at which everything works 99

→ SALE KIRKPATRICK,
writer and activist

FROM SCALE TO PROPORTIONALITY

We know that bigger can be too big. In fact, economists have a word for when it happens. They speak of "diseconomies of scale." When we look at questions of scale in social design we may rephrase the issue: when social economies of scale are out of proportion with regard to the human qualities and values they claim to serve, they turn into social diseconomies of scale. The sustainist perspective redirects our social design processes to questions of appropriate size and scale. It questions the (modernist) assumption that bigger is always better. Or that fast is better than slow. It challenges us to think in terms of appropriate scale and human dimensions. It shifts the focus of our social designs: from scale to proportionality.

THE VALUE OF PROPORTIONALITY: VARYING SPEED AND SIZE

Size matters. We know that bigger isn't always better. But neither can we simply follow E.F. Schumacher's adage that "small is beautiful." A sustainist perspective asks what scale is appropriate in a particular design. It questions the modernist ideas of large-scale as well as high speed. It asks us to proportion things, rather than following the principle of upscaling in size and speed as the only logic.

The prevailing idea of speed is an instructive example of how, in many of our design processes, we have become trapped in a modernist perspective of "faster=better." The concept of speed is a neutral entity in that it can be high or low, comparable to temperature or image resolution. High speed or low speed. Yet, when we think

of speed, we rarely think about the fact that it includes low speeds and slowness. Once we shift our perspective to issues of proportionality and appropriateness, we may avoid the upscaling trap.

APPROPRIATENESS AND HUMAN SCALE IN OUR DESIGN BRIEFS

The moment we abandon the idea of one-size-fits-all, we can address the issue of appropriateness. Hence, the first step in a proportional design strategy is to be sensitive to context. When small is better than large, and when it is not, depends on the situation. We need to assess when upscaling is the answer and when it isn't. Take the issue of high or low speed. Choosing between high or low speed needs to be posed as a design question. It is a strategic choice rather than an unquestioned assumption. It prompts us to raise questions about what the appropriate speed is in a given situation and when and where we need to bring selective slowness into our designs.

There is a series of social qualities and values behind the notion of "slow"—as in the "slow food movement"—that is relevant to designing for proportionality. When we speak of "slow food," "slow architecture" or "slow money," we are not just talking about the speed of things. It involves a certain mentality, sensibility, meaning, and a particular human experience that is implicit to slow design. It is clear that "slow living" implies a particular relationship to our environment and nature. By putting "slowness" on the table as a design criterion, we are steering the design process towards different attributes. Appropriate size as well as "selective slowness" become new social qualities that can be purposefully included in our design briefs.

PROPORTIONAL DESIGN

In practice, it may turn out to be relatively simple to assess what size and scale amounts to "proportional design." Often we don't need big size or large-scale when both users and producers are nearby. And not every design benefits from becoming a mass product. In social design, one-size-fits-all solutions often neglect what is happening in specific communities and contexts. What we are posing as a challenge, for both designers and non-designers, is to measure our social design solutions along a yardstick of proportionality. Artist-designers discovered the valued qualities of "limited editions" long ago. We can now extend that idea to social design.

The shift from scale to proportionality redirects our design strategies towards the human scale—with human needs and human relationships taking centre stage. While it is not easy to say what this will mean in practice, it does offer us a clear challenge: how may we include the design criterion of proportionality in our designs? We need to look closely at what different scales imply for social impact and social experiences. And, as is the case with all of the sustainist design qualities that we have addressed in this guide, it is essential that the issues of proportionality and appropriate scale are addressed right at outset of the design process—instead of at the end.

TO EXPLORE
ETSY.COM

Etsy is an online platform that sells small-scale, handmade goods. Within eight years it has grown into an online shop and shop window for more than half a million makers. Over ten million users have used the online shop, buying directly from producers that are making clothes, jewellery, sculptures, and more. The key to Etsy's success is its human scale: each maker is small enough to have a direct relationship with the buyer. The connections between producer and user are close. Often, the geographical distance is too. Etsy is designed for those who prefer a limited size. Upscaling would jeopardise its essential qualities.

VIEWPOINT
WENDELL BERRY, AMERICAN FARMER, POET AND ENVIRONMENTALIST

"You may need a large corporation to run an airline or to manufacture cars, but you don't need a large corporation to raise a chicken or a hog. You don't need a large corporation to process local food or local timber and market it locally."

Wendell Berry, Compromise, Hell!, in: *Orion Magazine*, November/December 2004

SUSTAINIST DESIGN PRACTICE

—

Twelve cases from a changing field

Encounters with **sustainist design in practice**

Design for social impact and design for sustainable innovation are not theoretical inventions, nor is sustainist design. Once we start looking at social design with our sustainist glasses on, we discover that sustainist design is all around us—although no one had called it by that name. With our design qualities at hand, we ask: **what are good examples of social design that demonstrate what sustainist design is all about?**

As part of the process of compiling this guide, we created an open web platform to bring together **illustrative sustainist design cases** (opensustainistdesign.net). In a collective effort, with and by the Amsterdam-based The Beach network for creative innovation, we sent a call out into the world to contribute and share examples. Meanwhile we surveyed our own surroundings, and beyond. In our search for social design cases in which sustainist qualities—such as sharing, localism, connectedness and proportionality—had already been put into practice we followed our intuitions, our professional insights, and our passions and built on our networks.

Our encounters and the contributions we received online offered us a great variety of social design cases to work with. In the pages that follow, we share a dozen examples. They are **sustainist designs avant la lettre**. Some are close to us, geographically or personally. Others come from far afield. They are not necessarily success stories, but tell of the bold initiatives of pioneers that are trying to create more liveable, sustainable, healthy, and socially just designs. In different domains and in different ways, they show us what is possible.

The designs and design approaches we present here are rich in diversity, but have a lot in common too. Each one of them has tens, if not hundreds, of counterparts all over the globe. Each of the dozen stories we are presenting here captures some of the essence of the **changing ethos in design** and of the **new sustainist values**. Together, they reveal how the nature and practice of social design is changing.

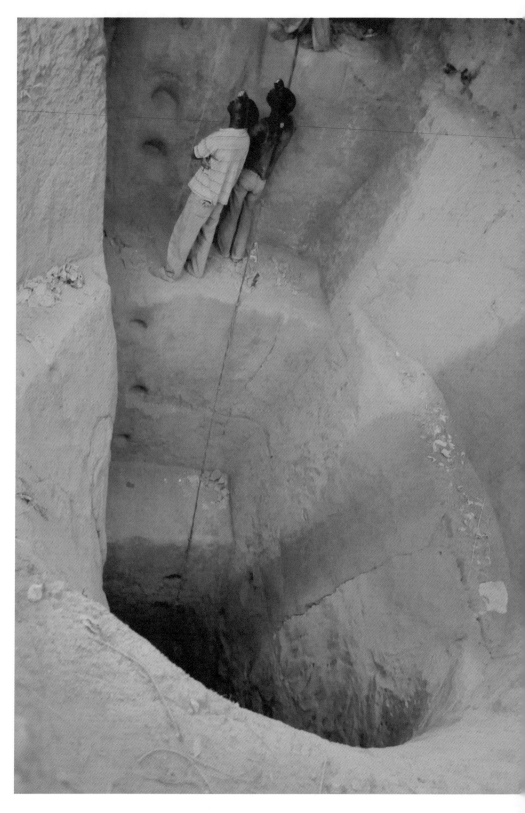

The mobile phone as change agent

Design activism at the heart of the production process

FairPhone is an initiative with an ambitious agenda. It aims to produce the world's first fair mobile phone: a mobile device that is being designed and produced while doing minimal harm to human beings or the environment. While on its journey, FairPhone is being confronted with all of the intricate complexities that the mobile phone production process and supply chain entail—many of which are anything but transparent and fair. FairPhone has the mission to once and for all open up the mobile phone industry's "ecosystem," from the extraction of raw materials to production, sales, and beyond.

"Companies tend to say that they have no way to backtrack more than three steps in their production chain," FairPhone founder Bas Van Abel says. "Therefore, it is a matter of disentangling the way in which the production process is built up. The phone itself is in fact the oracle that gives us access to understanding the system. That's why, at FairPhone, we take the actual mobile phone as our starting point. That's where we start contemplating about and designing our actions. Our original starting

↖ Miners in Katanga Province, Democratic Republic of the Congo. The hole goes 30 meters down into the ground where the cobalt ore can be found. From there, the creuseurs dig small tunnels to collect the ore. It takes approximately two months for a team of diggers to manually dig a hole like this. *Photo: FairPhone*

↑ This is the first prototype of FairPhone's fair mobile phone. It is designed according to Van Abel's design credo: "If you can't open it, you don't own it." *Photo: FairPhone*

↖↓ The 2012 edition of Dutch musical festival Lowlands hosted FairPhone as part of their festival programme. FairPhone invited festivalgoers to bring in their old mobile phones. By way of a recycling workshop, they gained insight into the amount of wasted precious materials that could have had a second life if extracted properly. No easy task: most of the devices proved to be tough nuts to crack. *Photo: FairPhone*

point for the design of a fair phone was an exercise in open design. Soon, we became aware of the fact that the system that makes mobile phone production possible is of a political nature. Which means that our design approach towards changing the system is in fact a form of design activism, aimed at opening up the system. Only if and when we take into account all aspects of the system—in a veritable holistic approach—we will be able to make progress."

Van Abel says he is fascinated by the complexity of the production system for mobile phones. "Alienation used to be an inherent characteristic of the way in which we designed our products, based on the ideal of efficiency in both production and distribution. That system was focused on the production of goods of a certain quality for a competitive price. In the information age, the virtues of the old system are decreasing in value quickly. Today, production is increasingly about generating and sharing knowledge and data together. As a designer, this puts you in charge of the system: designing is no longer about accepting alienation and complexity as a given, but about bringing different worlds together."

All-round fairness

When it comes to the production of the actual fair phone, the ultimate goal revolves around "fairness." Everything about the phone should qualify as fair: from the extraction of raw materials to the redevelopment of African mining sites and the safeguarding of labour conditions for manufacturers. This is required in order to be able to create a truly fair phone.

That's why FairPhone focuses on many things at once: it seeks alternative ways of acquiring the necessary raw materials by encouraging fair mining systems, it focuses on improving production and labour conditions, it emphasises "smart design" that is intended to last, it advocates for transparency in business deals, and promotes reuse and recycling.

Needless to say, this is easier said than done. Which is why FairPhone seeks collaboration with a variety of partners that are working on a diversity of issues. For example, FairPhone is part of the Conflict-Free Tin Initiative (CFTI) and the Solutions for Hope Project. Both initiatives aim to source conflict-free minerals in Congo. CFTI introduces a tightly controlled conflict-free supply chain outside the control

↑ Solutions for Hope miners at work in Katanga Province, Democratic Republic of the Congo. Miners here are being exploited, almost without exception. FairPhone is connecting with civil society organisations in the hopes of changing this. *Photo: FairPhone*

← Copper residue in Katanga Province, Democratic Republic of the Congo. Copper, one of the key metals that is used in the production of mobile phones, is everywhere. *Photo: FairPhone*

← A mobile phone shop with recharging facilities. As is the case in many other African countries, mobile phones have had an unmistakable impact on the infrastructure of the Congolese economy. Rural farmers, for example, can now consult with local traders to find out which market offers the best price for their products. *Photo: FairPhone*

of armed groups. Solutions for Hope is a similar project that was initiated by Motorola Solutions Inc. and the AVX Corporation, triggered by their own need for conflict-free materials, being large-scale users and processors of tantalum. Work is also being done to encourage fair gold from Peru. FairPhone is the first electronics manufacturer that is trying to incorporate fair trade gold in its products by setting up initiatives with FairTrade International (FLO) and the Alliance or Responsible Mining (ARM). Besides resolving mining-related issues, FairPhone also fosters better labour conditions in China by encouraging democratically elected worker unions and improved access to information. FairPhone strives to inspire existing industries by starting a movement for change.

A new ecosystem: "It's all about relationships"

"As time progressed," Van Abel explains, "FairPhone's goals became much bigger as we became aware that we need to stop tinkering with the issues in the production chain independently. We need to take a holistic approach and design an entirely new way of doing business in order to make it happen. At the same time, growth and profit are part of the deal, too, if we want to have a real impact."

Developing a market proposition and a business case was a necessary next step towards attracting investors and bringing the phone onto the market. FairPhone currently collaborates with organisations and companies that originate in the old system. Companies such as Vodafone

↑ FairPhone aims to assure better wages and improve working conditions. No child labour or hard labour may be involved in the production of its fair phone. *Photo: FairPhone*

↑ This mind map shows the economic structures and aspects of the production chain that FairPhone wants to positively influence. It uses a holistic approach and attempts to be aware of all aspects in the chain of production and consumption. *Photo: Unknown*

and KPN are employing brand managers and corporate social responsibility advisers that want their organisations to embrace new social and sustainable values. This means that there is potential within these types of organisations to change and fuel meaningful developments.

"As the mobile phone industry represents a circular economy in itself, FairPhone is actually marketing an altogether new ecosystem that we do not yet fully understand. It is a journey that we can all be a part of. The good news is that more and more people are excited to contribute: over 5,000 people have requested our fair phone already."

After running as a successful campaign at Waag Society for over two years, FairPhone was established as an independent social enterprise in January 2013. Pre-sales of its first model smart phone will commence mid-2013.

⊘ FAIRPHONE.ORG

SUSTAINIST DESIGN FEATURES

The FairPhone design and design process are sustainist all-round. FairPhone's overall aim: a real fair phone that takes into account social and sustainability attributes should be (made) possible. By no longer accepting the alienation and complexity that traditionally surround mobile phone production, the designer takes responsibility for changing the system.

→ FairPhone embraces the political nature of the design process. Its holistic approach includes the "design of the context" by challenging the conventional consumer electronics industry. It wants to restore the balance of what is appropriate by respecting human rights and promoting acceptable standards for workers that include a caring attitude towards our planet and the local environment.

→ The brand design reconnects users with nature, by creating awareness of the impact that the related demand for resources is having on people and the planet.

→ Due to the collaborative and networked nature of the design process, uncertainties abound. FairPhone accepts that it cannot control the design process and attempts to use the flow that is being generated to its best advantage.

 **SHARING**

Share to be fair is a motto that fits FairPhone well. Its effort is to overcome deficiencies in the system by sharing knowledge, skills, and information from mining to production to mobile phone use.

● **CONNECTEDNESS**

FairPhone (re)connects users with the product itself. Distinguishing itself from traditional mobile phone design, a fair phone can be opened by its users. So they can truly "own" it. Everyone is invited to participate in creative challenges on the FairPhone website, from designing your favourite phone to promoting the final product. FairPhone connects workers— miners, engineers, designers and producers —to business partners and consumers.

● **PROPORTIONALITY**

FairPhone's sensitivity to human scale is expressed by advocating for the rights of mine workers in Congo and Peru and production workers in China.

57

An end to land mines

Let's get it rolling

The **Mine Kafon**—<u>kafon</u> means explosion in Dari—is a landmine clearance solution that is designed by Massoud Hassani, an Afghan design student at Design Academy Eindhoven. As a child, he used to play in the Afghan desert where land mines claim many victims. As a designer, he combines this reality with the insights that he gained in his childhood. His Mine Kafon draws much attention from museums to design critics, and from engineers to NGOs that are interested in supporting the further development of Hassani's fresh approach to resolving life-threatening situations.

↓ *Photo: Hassani Design BV*

↑ The Mine Kafon is designed as a low-cost, wind-powered mine detonator that looks like a giant Dandelion-shaped ball. It is inspired by the handmade toys that designer Hassani and his friends made when they were kids growing up in Afghanistan. As a design student, Hassani began remaking the paper orbs of his youth in the hopes of being able to use them to detonate some of the ten million undetected mines that still cover his home country.

"On paper, Afghanistan is said to have ten million land mines. In reality, there are far, far more. Every destroyed land mine means a saved life and every life counts," Hassani explains. For the past sixty years, mine removal techniques have stayed largely the same. Often, it is local people that end up removing the mines. "A lot of people end up getting hurt."

A giant Dandelion-shaped ball

The Mine Kafon is a giant Dandelion-shaped ball that is made from bamboo and biodegradable plastics. When it rolls over a mine, it destroys itself as well as the landmine. Real-life testing with landmines has been done and has been documented in spectacular video reports. The current prototype is wind powered, but other forms of locomotion control of the Mine Kafon are currently being examined. The Mine Kafon's overall objective is two-fold: it should be safe and affordable. These are the core conditions for bringing the Mine Kafon to market.

Back in the day

"I grew up in Qasaba, Kabul. My family moved there when I was five years old, and at the time there were several wars going on. My brother Mahmud and I, we played every day on the fields that surrounded our neighbourhood," Hassani says. "When we were young we used to make our own toys. One of my favourites was a small rolling object that was wind powered. We used to race against the other kids in the fields around our neighbourhood. There was always a strong wind blowing towards the mountains. While we were racing against each other, our toys would roll too fast and too far. Mostly, they landed in areas where we couldn't go rescue them because of landmines. I still remember those toys I'd made that we lost and watching them just beyond where we could go."

Nearly twenty years later, Hassani used the memories of his childhood in Kabul and took to making the same toy once more. "I remade one, making it twenty times bigger, as well as heavier and stronger," he states. "Powered by the wind, it's meant for the same areas which were, and still are, full of mines."

← Mine Kafon being put to the test at Explosive Ordnance Disposal at De Riel, the Netherlands. The wind-powered detonator proved to be up for a series of four explosions before being ready for replacement. *Photo: Hassani Design BV*

Resonance within society

Hassani's Mine Kafon is resonating powerfully in the public debate on the value and ethics of design. In what is essentially an open design process, the whole world is now looking over his shoulder while he develops the product. This openness invites criticism. The designer is being attacked by critics that are questioning the effectiveness of his Mine Kafon. What if the product does not actually clear all mines in a given area? What if there is no wind? How do you control the movement of the deminer?

When we apply a new outlook on what it means to be a designer, the fundamental changes that are reshaping design culture are clearly manifested in Hassani's approach. His project represents the design process of the future:

the deminer is being developed in an open and collaborative process. And the process moves slowly. Instead of rushing through the prototyping phase, Hassani is taking his time to take in all of the criticisms and use them towards optimising the Mine Kafon. With the help of some of the one thousand engineers and other supporters that offered their expertise, in addition to a crowd funded budget of over 100,000 Euros, Hassani intends to bring the product to the next level before collaborating with parties that are part of the more traditional mine clearing business. His design process is human-centred and deliberately uses the attention that is being generated towards improving his product.

⊙ MINEKAFON.BLOGSPOT.NL

↗ The Moroccan dessert was chosen as the first testing ground outside of the Netherlands to examine the movement of the Mine Kafon. Under circumstances that are in many ways similar to those in Afghanistan, the Mine Kafon was assembled by locals to test its usability. *Photo: Hassani Design BV*

↑ Hassani acknowledges the limitations of wind-powered locomotion. In his studio, a follow-up model is being designed after testing and debating the first prototype. It contains small engines and a metal detection unit.
Photo: Hasani Design BV

SUSTAINIST DESIGN FEATURES

The design of Mine Kafon brings together a range of sustainist design qualities. Hassani's perspective is that of an insider. The designer's real-life experience with the situation in Afghanistan adds value to the design of the deminer. Furthermore, his design shows how children's play, locally based experience and the unexpected can be a source of inspiration in social design. The personal engagement of the designer fuels his persistence to contribute to resolving the problem of land mines.

→ Mine Kafon emphasises the value of branding as a social design strategy: the designer works transparently and makes use of the attention that is being generated by the media to showcase his photogenic demining device to a large audience. This dynamic becomes a dominant quality of the design process.

→ Mine Kafon demonstrates the value of collaborative development and community building. As a result of the overall attention that has been generated for Hassani's deminer, a large amount of money was crowd funded and hundreds of experts have offered their skills and knowledge to improve Hassani's prototype.

● **LOCALISM**

Characteristic local circumstances sparked the idea of the Mine Kafon and provide it with meaning. Additionally, the testing efforts in a Moroccan desert explicitly involved the local community, thereby acknowledging the importance of localism.

● **CONNECTEDNESS**

Media attention and crowd funding are being used as important components of the design process. Relationships with experts have resulted.

● **PROPORTIONALITY**

Hassani is taking his time while designing the Mine Kafon. As a result, he is in a position to determine the process carefully and to only include partners if and when it is relevant to the process.

Poo in the loo

Hands down, the best way to prevent diarrhoea

Worldwide, 2.6 billion persons—that's four out of ten people—live without access to adequate sanitation. Due to a lack of toilets and proper hygiene, flies, feet, and fingers carry hazardous bacteria and viruses that are transferred from faeces into food and water. The diarrhoea that results is one of the leading causes of child death among the poorest of the world. It is the biggest killer of children under five years of age and takes more lives than HIV/AIDS, malaria, and measles combined. But just installing toilets does not solve the problem. According to **WASH United** it is essential to change people's mindsets first, because only a wanted toilet is a toilet that actually gets used and is kept clean. Equally important is proper hand-washing behaviour as hand-washing with soap is by far the most effective way to prevent diarrhoea.

WASH United:
a club that promotes wellbeing

That's why Thorsten Kiefer, human rights lawyer and devout football fan, founded WASH United. "[I am] driven by the vision of a world in which all people can talk openly about toilets, shit and shitting, in which toilets and hygiene are cool and relevant, and in which all people enjoy the safety and dignity of a toilet and practice good hygiene," Kiefer explains. That's why WASH United is not just another civil society organisation. Rather, it positions itself as a club that unites some of the world's biggest athletes with school children in Africa and India, as well as political decision makers, and people around the world. United, they make an effort to advance access to safe drinking water, sanitation, and hygiene for all people, everywhere.

Together with a coalition of international and local civil society organisations, United Nations agencies, governments, and leading actors from the world of sports, WASH United aims to create excitement around the neglected issues of global sanitation and hygiene. It makes use of interactive games, superstar role models, and a healthy dose of fun to fundamentally change mindsets around the "dirty" issues of sanitation and hygiene and to facilitate behavioural change.

Joining hands to make hand washing "cool and sexy"

WASH United is designed as a brand that brings together the world of WASH (Water, Sanitation and Hygiene) with the world of football and taps right into the powerful visual language of

↖ A Kenyan child shows a poster of Ivory Coast soccer player Didier Drogba explaining the importance of maintaining hygiene. *Photo: WASH United*

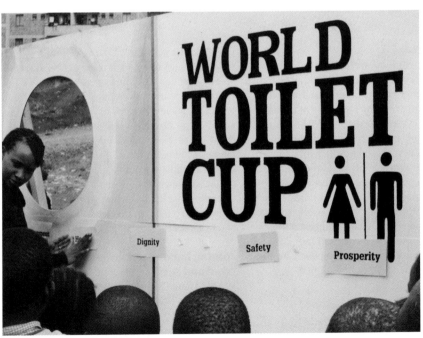

← Playing World Toilet Cup in Tanzania. WASH United teams up with African and international football stars, who act as champions for safe drinking water, sanitation and hygiene. WASH United harnesses the power of sports through football-based games to raise awareness of the importance of these issues.
Photo: WASH United

↓ Handy and Soapy are best friends and function as WASH United mascots. They perform during the half-time break.
Photo: Christian Klant/ WASH United

professional football clubs—with its own code of arms, team shirts, and club rules. Similar to big football clubs like Manchester United, WASH United creates strong emotions of togetherness and a sense of identity among its members. In addition, it reinforces the commitment of club members to adhere to the WASH rules, which form the foundation of membership to the WASH United club. That's how WASH United has become much more than just a project.

The medium is the message

The initial WASH United campaign leading up to the 2010 FIFA World Cup in South Africa reached more than 25 million people. WASH United's positive football-based communication has opened up completely new media channels for WASH topics. Major magazines as well as mainstream television broadcasts now raise WASH-related topics due to the appeal of associated international sports stars.

Within the first year of campaigning, the WASH United club had already grown to some 32,000 members, most of whom joined through

↖ On its journey through ← India, WASH United introduced a board game. Kanchey or marbles is a popular game here, especially in the rural parts of the country. In the WASH United version of the game, each player aims to get his poo pieces into the loo first. *Photo: Himanshu Khagta/WASH United and Sonja Och/ WASH United*

↑ Poo Minefield became one of the most popular carnival games at the Nirmal Bharat Yatra. Here, entertainer MC Maddy watches as a blindfolded player is guided through the minefield by the rest of his team. Using only verbal commands, the players have to ensure that their blindfolded teammate navigates the minefield without coming into contact with "poo mines." *Photo: Sonja Och/WASH United*

WASH school programmes. These programmes educate children and teachers in a fun and participatory way about the importance of safe drinking water, sanitation, and hygiene to facilitate life-saving behavioural changes.

Focus on continuous innovation

According to Kiefer, WASH United has been design-focused and innovation-driven from day one. "We work with some great agencies [Südfeuer in Germany and Studio Miscellanea in India] and we simply love coming up with new beautiful out-of-the-box solutions to promote sanitation and hygiene." WASH United developed and tested more than twenty new stall and arena games—including *Poo Minefield*, which turns out to be a real blockbuster. In this game, blindfolded contestants must rely on voice commands to get through an open defecation zone and pick up soap bars for bonus points. In Kenya, WASH United is about to start a new project in which it collaborates with street artists from informal settlements to get sanitation and hygiene messaging out into their communities.

Project partners

WASH United is supported by a wide range of international partners that include international and local civil society organisations, United Nations agencies, governments, and leading figures from the world of football. In the target countries, WASH United activities are carried out with and by local partner organisations (both non-governmental and governmental), international partners' country offices, and within WASH networks. WASH United currently works with approximately one hundred local organisations and networks that implement activities in the field.

WASH United is supported by a wide range of international donors, including the German Federal Foreign Office, the Swiss Agency for Development Cooperation, the German Organisation for Development Cooperation (GIZ), and many more.

⊙ **WASH-UNITED.ORG**

↑ Entertainer MC Maddy is playing musical toilets with a girl at the Great WASH Yatra in the town of Indore. When the music stops, each player must find a toilet to sit on. In each round, the one person that is left standing without a toilet is disqualified. *Photo: Himanshu Khagta/WASH United*

SUSTAINIST DESIGN FEATURES

Building interconnections based on mutual trust and creating small-scale shared experiences are essential features of sustainist design. WASH United embraces these elements in its design process. Its main purpose is to build relationships that will ultimately create a movement of sanitation-related change.

→ We may view WASH United's effort as the design of a collective experience or a situation —called a club—where form follows meaning.

→ The collaborative spirit and inspiring con-tributions of role models create a new kind of reso-nance around sanitation matters. Playful inter-ventions during festivals engage more people and invite them to join in.

→ WASH United uses the design of a brand, events, and games to collectively change the mindsets of local communities in India and Africa. Therefore, it can be seen as an act of "design activism."

● SHARING

The visual power of the graphics and events are attractive for mass media to share with the world, which has proven to be instrumental to building a community with a cause.

● LOCALISM

Hazardous hygiene situ-ations can only be solved by changing mindsets and behaviour on community level. To this end, local celebrities function as role models for sanitary be-haviour at local community events.

● CONNECTEDNESS

The visual rhetoric of football and the related sense of club identity attract and connect the young and old. The shared symbol (the brand) ties the many into a large and powerful movement. Binding people together functions as a strong and effective tactic to (collec-tively) overcoming shame.

Savouring the local

Creating community through the art of brewing

The mobile **Outside Brewery** installation was developed by designer Henriëtte Waal as a way to highlight the culture of home brewing and reconnect the brewing process to the landscape. Waal perceives the actual skill of brewing to be a vital aspect of her design process. In her design projects, she makes an effort to actually learn a new skill herself that will allow her to become part of a specific subculture. "This method makes it possible to work from the inside out as a designer," she explains. In the case of the Outside Brewery, collecting and organising knowledge and expertise on the craft, culture and location of beer brewing is her contribution to uniting different worlds, and developing new tastes together—literally.

← Designer Henriëtte Waal's Outside Brewery uses an ingenious system of kettles and tubes to supply the DAG HAP Festival in the city of The Hague with locally brewed beer that consists of ditch water and a mix of wild plants and herbs.
Photo: Arenda Oomen

← In and around the city of Tilburg, over fifty amateur brewers are brewing homemade beer in their garages. Together, they are producing around 15,000 litres of beer annually. Jointly, they designed the Outside Brewery installation.

Designer Henriëtte Waal took on the Outside Brewery project in order to expose the culture and skills of amateur brewers. Rainwater and wild plants from the surrounding area are used as ingredients to the "landscape beer." This reconnects the brewers to the local landscape.
Photo: Ralph Kämena

Rainwater and wild plants from the surrounding area function as signature ingredients to the unique brand of "landscape beer" (*Landschaps-bier*) that is produced by the installation. By using water from local ditches and heating, cooking, filtering, flavouring and fermenting it, the Outside Brewery essentially makes a place or a landscape "drink-able" in the form of a beer. Since the start of the project in 2009, beer has been brewed in different locations around the Netherlands, producing a series of one-of-a-kind local brews. In the process, Waal developed some fine brewing skills of her own and even became a certified beer judge.

Co-designing an outside brewery

The Outside Brewery was originally developed in the framework of the cultural programme "Eat-able Landscape" (*Eetbaar Landschap*)

that was hosted by the city of Tilburg in 2009. In and around the city of Tilburg alone, there are more than fifty amateur home brewers. Their makeshift breweries tend to be located in sheds and garages. They jointly produce an estimated 15,000 litres of beer annually. Waal mobilised these home brewers. They got to know each other and their surroundings in a special way. The joint design of the Outside Brewery followed, producing litres of Klavertje Bier from using the locally abundant red clover (*Trifolium pratense*) as its primary ingredient.

Ingredients: malt, water, and herbs

Water retrieved from a nearby ditch or pond is purified in a filtering tower. The filtering construction consists of a used paper container, a fluid container, as well as individual water bottles. Each of the containers holds a different

filter, but all of them are made of natural materials. The paper container holds a filter that is made of ceramics. The other filters use coal as well as sand in other to purify the water. After the filtering process is finished, Waal uses the water to brew beer by adding malt and—most importantly—a mix of locally harvested herbs that is used to add a distinct taste.

Life at the local brewery
Different landscapes generate different local ingredients, which in turn generate different local beer recipes. "As designers, we are usually hosted by a given landscape without knowing very much about its specific qualities," Waal says. She refers to the French concept of terroir, which can be loosely translated as "a sense of place," and which represents the interaction between unique local characteristics that are expressed in agricultural products. At the core of the concept is the assumption that the land from which the product has grown imparts a unique quality that is specific to that growing site. The geography, geology and climate of a certain place all play their part in it. "In order to truly understand the local, you need to collaborate with the locals," she adds. "I always feel the need to go local myself."

New local beers have surfaced, carrying meaningful names such as Rotterdam Snow Beer (*Rotterdams Sneeuwbier*), Sloterplas Blond Beer (*Sloterplas Blond*), Clover Beer (*Klavertje Bier*), and Rotsoord Beer (*Rotsoord Bier*). During the Amsterdam Sloterplas Festival in 2010, the Outside Brewery brewed Sloterplas Blond Beer, which is a clear beer made of water from Sloterplas Lake and has a naturally low alcohol percentage of only 3%.

The Outside Brewery is a mobile installation capable of travelling. Additionally, designer Waal offers brewing workshops—she terms them "beer education"—so as to make sure that people continue to have a sense of what they are actually drinking. And to safeguard this valuable Dutch cultural product from extinction.

➲ HENRIETTEWAAL.NL/SITE.PHP?ID=8

➲ RENT-A-PROJECT.COM/PROJECTEN/347/
BUITENBROUWERIJ

← Gathered herbs, flowers and berries function as ingredients to "ditch water beer."
Photo: Jorn van Eck

SUSTAINIST DESIGN FEATURES

The design process for making "landscape beer" unites a range of sustainist elements. It emphasises the sharing of skills, raises environmental awareness, encourages appreciation of local place and natural resources, and builds community.

→ **The Outside Brewery, as a designed meeting place and local laboratory for brewing, connects crafts to the local context and terroir, whilst using natural ingredients in the beer making process.**

→ **By combining these elements it goes well beyond functional design, it creates meaning and experience that is part of the flavour of the product, quite literally.**

● LOCALISM

The local character of the project is essential to it. The fundamental ingredients of the "landscape beer"—from the water to the skills—are all local. The design enhances a sense of place, because both its meaning and experience are locally rooted. As a result, the Outside Brewery, the beer, and its taste become part of the local cultural heritage.

● CONNECTEDNESS

A community is built around the skills of beer making in a local context. It connects people by the exchange of skills and the joint design of a local beer.

Relationships are one of the primary outcomes of the design: tasting events connect local beer lovers—both producers and consumers—to each other and to their natural environment.

● PROPORTIONALITY

The success of the design results from its limited scale. The resources and ingredients are close by and producing on the spot naturally gives the product a human scale. Small-scale local production, which is deliberately designed for an exclusive market only, is an essential attribute. It gives this beer, and the experience of drinking it, a unique quality.

↑ Participants taste the beer that resulted from the brewing workshops during the DAG HAP festival in the city of The Hague, the Netherlands.
Photo: Jorn van Eck

→ The mobile Outside Brewery with the water treatment plant in the background in the city of The Hague, the Netherlands. A temporary beer academy offered people the opportunity to learn the art of brewing. The collective brewing that ensued could be interpreted as a tool for urban development.
Photo: Jorn van Eck

Urban resilience in a time of change

Shifting ground in a Parisian suburb

Agrocité is an urban agriculture programme in the suburb of Colombes, which is an underprivileged town of 84,000 inhabitants near the city of Paris. The pilot programme that started in early 2012 is designed to introduce the dynamics of urban agriculture to community life. This will reconnect neighbours to one another and their living environment, empower them, and help revitalise a neglected urban context. The project includes a micro-experimental farm, community gardens, educational and cultural spaces, and devices for energy production, composting and rainwater recycling.

Agrocité is part of a wider effort, called R-Urban, that encourages networks of urban resilience in European cities. R-Urban is a concept by Atelier d'Architecture Autogérée. It envisions the bottom-up development of urban resilience, cultivating the ability of urban systems to adapt and thrive in changing circumstances. It involves the creation of a network of locally closed ecological cycles that link a series of urban activities together. "To overcome the current crisis we must try to produce what we consume and consume what we produce," Atelier d'Architecture Autogérée explains. Within the R-Urban project, this chain of production and consumption is interpreted well beyond the material aspects of it, and also includes the cultural, cognitive, and affective dimensions of production and consumption.

Small interventions to tackle big themes

Small pioneering interventions are designed to tackle big social and ecological themes. New collective solidarity-based practices come into being through co-workership of neighbours and professionals. These new practices include ecological approaches such as reduce, reuse and recycle, or iterations as repair, re-design, re-think, and re-assemble. But it does not stop there. Environmental issues (CO_2 reduction, waste recycling, ecological footprint reduction) and social, economic and cultural issues (re-skilling, job creation, diverse economies) are addressed, too.

At present, R-Urban is testing how democratic and bottom–up processes of resilient regeneration work in a suburban context so that future strategies for change may be adapted to

↖ A new, shared space
← is being developed
by local citizens amidst
old and new buildings in
the suburb of Colombes,
near Paris. *Photo: Atelier
d'Architecture Autogérée*

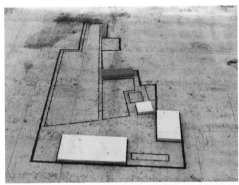

← Model showing a rough lay out of the gardens. *Photo: Atelier d'Architecture Autogérée*

→ Infographic explaining how the civic, agricultural, cultural and pedagogical units will function. *Source: AgroCité*

↖ A co-design session with people from the neighbourhood investigates the functioning of Agrocité. *Photo: Atelier d'Architecture Autogérée*

↑ Agrocité, viewed from one of the newly built residential towers. *Photo: Atelier d'Architecture Autogérée*

→ In the background, the community house is being built. A seed library, a vegetable market, a collective café, a workshop and a pedagogical unit will host a range of activities. *Photo: Atelier d'Architecture Autogérée*

this. "No radical change will happen in current society without the involvement of the many," Atelier d'Architecture Autogérée argues. That's why the R-Urban concept is explicitly designed for the purpose of appropriation by others. A growing group of neighbours in the Colombes area is already applying the concept to affecting real change in their living environment.

From the local to the regional

R-Urban explores the possibilities of enhancing the capacity of urban resilience by a network of resident-run facilities. Here, complementarities between different fields of activity are being created, be they economic, agricultural, social, or cultural. Workshops are offered that teach participants how to work with stock materials, such as reclaimed wood, that they collect themselves in the surrounding areas throughout the year. This kind of collaborative local production supports the emergence of alternative models of living, producing, and consuming between the urban and the rural.

Examples of alternative production and consumption are manifold. In Colombes, surplus vegetables are being recycled into compost for farmland or heating. Rainwater is being collected for "aquaponics"—which is a sustainable food production system that combines traditional aquaculture with hydroponics in a symbiotic environment—to serve the local food economy. An example of regional collaboration is R-Urban's cooperation with the Clinamen Association. The association aims to increase the dynamics in the urban territory by promoting agricultural practices that originate in the countryside. Led by their shepherd, Olivier Marcouyoux, the association seeks to provide a place for animals in urban areas to allow city dwellers to remain in touch with the culture of their ancestors.

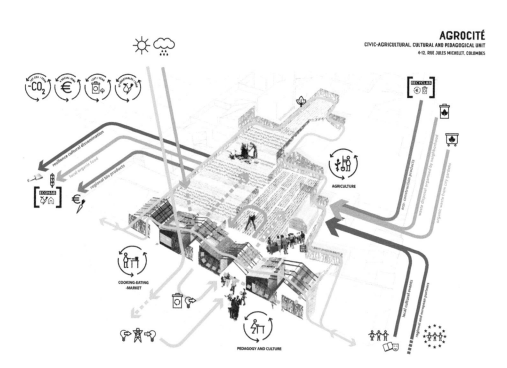

RECYCLAB

AGRICULTURE

eco-construction products

waste disposal organised by neighbourhood

organic waste from city gardens

resilience cultural dissemination

local organic food

regional bio products

ECOHAB

COOKING-EATING
-MARKET

local cultural events

regional and european partners

PEDAGOGY AND CULTURE

↑ The whole community gets involved, youngsters as well as the elderly.
Photo: Atelier d'Architecture Autogérée

↑ Neighbours are gathering around a tasty vegetable soup made with local products grown in the experimental agricultural plots. All leftovers are being composted.
Photo: Atelier d'Architecture Autogérée

Collective Ownership

Agrocité works as a network, too. The network shares cultivable land that includes an experimental urban agricultural farm, a shared garden for neighbourhood residents, an educational garden, and a shared greenhouse for plants and seedlings. The buildings include prototypes for organic intensive farming. There is a seed library, a vegetable market with local agricultural products, a collective café, a cooking facility, and a collective bread oven. The R-Urban cooperative land trust consists of founding members who manage the land. In this way, they try to find a collective answer to the problem of financial access to land—while at the same time reinventing collective practices and uses of the city, in addition to being responsible environmentally and showing social solidarity.

⬢ R-URBAN.NET/EN/PROJECTS/AGROCITE

⬢ R-URBAN.NET/EN/ACTIVITIES

↑ Waste materials are collected in the surrounding areas throughout the year to be used for the building of Agrocité. The use of recycled materials demands altogether different construction practices.
Photo: K. Trogal

SUSTAINIST DESIGN FEATURES

The small-scale, context-specific and engaging approach of this "eco-urban resilience" design project qualifies as sustainist design because it strengthens the bottom-up empowerment of the people living in the suburb of Colombes. Small pioneering interventions fuel new collective practices that aim for ecological, social, economic, and cultural transition simultaneously. This increases the local community's resilience. Agrocité contributes to the networked movement of R-Urban, which is growing quickly by sharing knowledge with other (distributed) projects. It focuses indirectly on the power of local, small-scale, yet deeply rooted co-design.

● SHARING

The food that is produced is not owned by anyone, but by everyone—just like the land, the equipment to cultivate it, and the buildings. Everything is owned by the collective and managed by a cooperative land trust.

● LOCALISM

Agrocité is creating a (physical) local base and a sense of place by combining small-scale food production and peer-to-peer education in a local situation. It transforms an undefined public space into a commons by inviting neighbours to examine the qualities that are at hand within their community.

● CONNECTEDNESS

People connect to nature and crafts by going there themselves. In the workshops that are offered by R-Urban, they become reconnected and they (re)discover that "making things" is a way to master their own lives. The design process is participative and open to anyone. It is inclusive and connects professionals and amateurs, young and old, and people from various cultural backgrounds.

● PROPORTIONALITY

The R-Urban strategy and Agrocité programme is defined by the principle that we should "produce what we consume, and consume what we produce."

Craftsmanship with benefits

Restoring lives, crafts, and the environment

Lamon Luther is a United States company that designs and builds furniture from reclaimed materials. Its employees are skilled craftsmen who were forced into homelessness during the recent recession. Lamon Luther's mission is manifold: it is about keeping craftsmanship alive, creating hope and opportunity for homeless carpenters, as well as reusing of reclaimed materials.

Talent in the woods

In 2008, the American economy had come to a grinding halt. Many talented people in the building industry lost their jobs. Over time, they lost their homes, families and dignity. Some of them were carpenters and ended up being homeless. Brian Preston, founder of Lamon Luther, learned about a community of homeless people living in a makeshift camp in the woods near his home in the state of Georgia. Wanting to help, he became acquainted with the homeless and soon became aware that simply donating supplies was not going to structurally change their prospects for the better. They needed jobs and an opportunity to provide for themselves. At the time, Preston was working as creative director, designing graphics and doing photography. But being a craftsman at heart, he longed for his carpentering. He decided to give his dream a shot and started off hiring

← Former homeless craftsmen at work in the Lamon Luther workshop in Douglasville, Georgia. *Photo: Micah Beardan*

the men to work in a carpentry workshop. He picked up Roger Anthony Curtis from the camp and brought him to a workshop to see whether his carpentry skills were still good after years of wandering around homeless. He was pleasantly surprised by what he saw and eventually hired two more men from the camp and another who was living in a trailer. He decided to found a custom design-build carpentry business with these men as the crew. Soon, Curtis and the others had saved up enough money to move out of the woods into a group home.

Keeping the tradition of craftsmanship alive

The concept proved to be a success and a full-blown carpentry business soon followed. All of the current carpenters have become financially independent enough to move out of the woods and into apartments. As the business continues to grow, they will continue to find homeless men to hire. "In the current economic climate, there are many skilled workers out there who need a job. Finding them and connecting them to our work will not be a challenge," Lamon Luther

↑ Constructing gigantic type out of scrap wood. Using recycled materials is at the core of the Lamon Luther philosophy. From shipping pallets to old barns to recycled metals, everything is used in the construction of Lamon Luther products. *Photo: Micah Beardan*

founder Preston states. Since the start of their business, they have hired only one person who was not homeless to handle logistics.

First and foremost, Lamon Luther wants to be a tribute to the American craftsman. Being a craftsman is a calling, according to the company. That's why it equips these craftsmen-in-need with the tools that they once loved, thereby keeping alive the tradition of American craftsmanship that is disappearing with each generation.

Every piece of furniture tells a story

Reclaimed and repurposed materials are used in all Lamon Luther creations. They create an art of picking and selecting specific materials that capture the essence of the process. They rescue and restore anything from shipping pallets to old barns to recycled metals. Lamon Luther builds its products with materials that would otherwise end up in landfills and every finished product is unique and one-of-a-kind. A table is more than just a table: it's a place where memories will be made for years to come. Lamon Luther hopes that consumers will pass its handcrafted products down, which is why they are built to last longer than a lifetime.

The new philanthropy

The workshop is growing quickly. There's an ongoing flow of custom orders coming in. That's why Lamon Luther is now looking at renovating an old warehouse into an expansive new facility in order to keep up with the amount of work. The goal is not to scale the company to something that loses the personal nature of its story. Nonetheless, they do intend to grow so that they can help restore and train more and more craftsmen, as well as produce more and more quality products.

Lamon Luther is a free enterprise on a mission. "The perception is that you can't do good while being a free enterprise," Preston says. However, he believes that the modern-day consumer is increasingly interested in free enterprise that gives back, that does good, and creates good. "I think we are sending a message to the world that says: this is the new philanthropy. It's okay to make money and do good."

→ EDITION.CNN.COM/2012/10/03/LIVING/
LAMON-LUTHER-TEDXATLANTA

Lamon Luther is an example of sustainist design because it combines bottom-up development, local rootedness, and making "more with less" by turning waste materials into unique pieces of furniture. Lamon Luther is not invented and implemented in a top-down manner. Rather, it has come into being as a result of the talents that were available. They jointly shape the company. Passion, enthusiasm, and empathy are its instigators.

→ Lamon Luther's founding designer aimed to combine his passion for craftsmanship with doing good. His company is now creating context-specific social value in the form of local business with additional benefits on different levels.

→ Lamon Luther is more than just a company: it represents a community that is rediscovering the value of the local and of craftsmanship. The collective makers culture and the sharing of expertise is used to imbue the community with meaning.

→ The Lamon Luther workshop qualifies as a designed environment— a situation—that exemplifies restoration in every way: it restores craftsmanship, it reuses local materials, and it shares knowledge and expertise related to carpentry and local style and culture.

● SHARING

The collaborative effort of making a complete new business can only be done by the peer-to-peer process of sharing knowledge and collectively developing skills.

● LOCALISM

The value of local resources and materials is being addressed. The craftsmen are connected to their direct living environment and they use the local resources thoughtfully. As a result, each piece of furniture that is produced by Lamon Luther carries its own meaningful story. The craftsmen as well as the products reflect a sense of place.

● CONNECTEDNESS

Making furniture makes the craftsmen visible and reconnects them to society, to each other, and to themselves, by strengthening their skills and self-confidence.

● PROPORTIONALITY

Inherent to the business model is rescuing and restoring reclaimed materials. Less scrap goes to landfills and the initial production cost goes down. The rediscovery of human energy as a resource shows how values are shifting from costly mass production to small-scale production of "limited edition" pieces of furniture with a story.

↓ *Photo: Micah Beardan*

Sharing energy

Building the world's next power network from the ground up

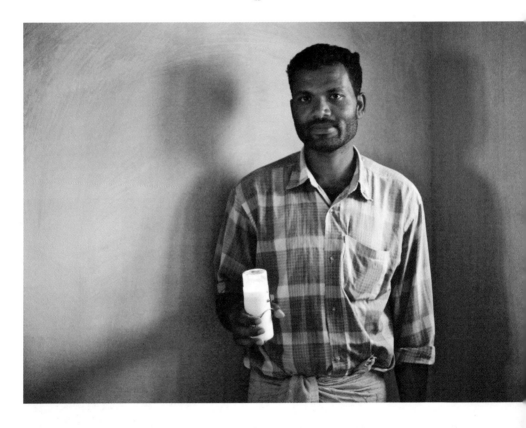

In theory, plenty of sustainable energy is available, powered by the sun, water, or the wind. Yet, this energy is hard to control, which is why it fails to structurally meet our needs. **Rural Spark** contributes to resolving this problem by designing smart grids that are owned by distributed local energy networks. They link supply and demand in a smart way, thereby enabling local communities to sell and buy surpluses more easily—while generating all sorts of social advantages on the side.

It is Rural Spark's ambition to encourage smart grids, specifically in developing countries, enabling their citizens to leapfrog traditional top-down, centralised energy grids. "Rural Spark empowers local stakeholders to grow an autonomous functioning network, in which energy, information, maintenance, and profits are distributed on all levels, thereby actively participating in the growth of an open, new world energy market from the bottom-up," it sums up its mission.

Villagers turned entrepreneurs

Rural Spark has taken on the challenge to shape the distributed energy networks of the future, starting in rural India. By way of an iterative method, it develops special kits that allow local villagers to generate energy themselves. The context-specific kit includes something that can function as their energy source. Depending on the setting, this may come in the form of a solar panel or a tiny hydroelectric power station. The kit also includes an energy router that enables the villager to channel the energy and share it with his fellow villagers in return for a small fee. It turns him or her

into a veritable entrepreneur overnight: fellow villagers will drop off their chargeable items in the morning and retrieve them in the evening, along with having a cup of tea and discussing the local news. These village-level entrepreneurs make a tangible difference in their communities, while earning both money and social status for themselves.

Rural Spark takes responsibility for the relatively high costs of setting up the system's infrastructure, while local entrepreneurs pay a monthly subscription fee that ensures proper local maintenance of the network, continuity and reliability. Although the traditional source of energy in rural India—kerosene and firewood —is relatively cheap, the sun, the wind, and water are ultimately sources of energy that come free of charge. Also, they are safe, clean, and sustainable. That's how the initial investment that is required to become part of the Rural Spark energy network pays off quickly and on different levels.

There's more

On sunny days, energy suppliers that make use of a solar panel are able to generate far more energy than they actually need. To capture this energy, Rural Spark has introduced *Share Cubes* that enable an entrepreneur to store surplus energy. In this way, surplus energy is no longer wasted but, instead, it can be traded on an emerging market of supply and demand. On a windy but cloudy day, an entrepreneur that makes use of wind-powered energy can

← Meet Mr. Ranjit. In his position as local energy supplier, he serves an important role in the Indian town of Sankuhi, as well as in the overall distributed energy network. His newly installed solar panel offers him access to energy that he can then use to charge mobile phones and LED lamps—his own as well as others'. The energy network exists by virtue of small local entrepreneurs like Mr. Ranjit who, by taking responsibility for their own small part, essentially take responsibility for the functioning of the whole network. *Photo: Rural Spark*

↓ These LED lamps are produced at a very low cost price, which makes a big difference to poor households. They can be recharged at the indoor charging stations of local entrepreneurs. *Photo: Rural Spark*

sell his surplus to his fellow entrepreneurs that are depending on the power of the sun. By the exchange of energy surpluses, a reliable distributed network is taking shape that is able to accommodate both supply and demand in a far cheaper way than centralised, top-down energy networks are able to do.

↑ Installing a solar panel on Mr. Ranjit's roof during the pilot project in and around Jabalpur (Madhya Pradesh, India). *Photo: Rural Spark*

Design in context

"Many products are being developed in a far-away lab and do not actually accommodate the local context, because they do not take into account the many stakeholders and factors that influence local culture," co-initiator Van Heist says. That's why Rural Spark makes an effort to actually physically move into the local situation and to design on the spot—in an explicitly demand-driven way. To this end, an agile design process is used with short feedback cycles, from Research & Development to implementation in the field. This allows for a process of rapid prototyping within the local situation that involves all stakeholders.

Opportunity through scarcity

Currently, approximately 400 million rural Indians are living without access to electricity. The gap between the quality of life of the urban rich and the rural poor is widening. In spite of

↑ The complete Rural Spark starter kit. One solar panel generates enough energy to light seven lamps. *Photo: Rural Spark*

the dim circumstances of many rural Indians, Rural Spark views their current situation as an opportunity. The sheer lack of infrastructure that currently exists offers the opportunity to start fresh. That's why Rural Spark leaves the beaten track of top-down government intervention. Instead, it directly involves the people themselves, offering them responsibility, direct returns, and livelihood.

Bottom-up community building

Besides economic and environmental benefits, the bottom-up sharing of energy is proving to have vast social effects on the village level. For the empowered entrepreneur, it increases ownership. Also, social cohesion increases between all stakeholders involved. This provides an extra social incentive to both the consumer and the entrepreneur to take care of the system, ensuring its continuation. Together, the villagers are using solar energy in an altogether new way, enhancing the feeling of community and collective responsibility.

RURALSPARK.COM/SHARE/TRUE_ ENTREPRENEURSHIP.PDF

SUSTAINIST DESIGN FEATURES

The combination of sustainable innovation and social design is at the heart of sustainist design. Rural Spark designs for small-scale empowerment in order to ultimately bring about a sustainable revolution in the way we use energy. It envisions a bottom-up network approach to build local communities around energy from which all individuals involved benefit directly.

● SHARING

The bottom-up sharing of energy (via *Share Cubes*) and open exchange of information offers direct rewards, both material (electricity or an income) and immaterial (social connections, community building).

● PROPORTIONALITY

By the exchange of energy surpluses, a reliable distributed network is taking shape that is able to accommodate both supply and demand in a far cheaper way than large-scale, centralised, top-down energy networks are able to do.

↑ Lighting marks the difference between boredom and ignorance and social interaction, learning and empowerment. The LED lamps are a good replacement for the smelly and dangerous kerosene lamps. *Photo: Rural Spark*

WE ARE HERE

Konakry
guinee accra

ABIDJAN
zyalé
cote d'ivoire

sierra leone
masao

Oromy

eritrea

khat toher
sudan

Coming closer

Placemaking by undocumented refugees

The **We Are Here** project was triggered by the 2012 eviction of refugees from a refugee centre in Ter Apel, a small village near the German border in the northeast of the Netherlands. Asylum seekers from Somalia, Eritrea, Ethiopia, Sudan, Kenya, Congo, Mauritania, Ivory Coast, Sierra Leone, Mali, Guinea, and Iraq were denied residency in the Netherlands and, as a result, evicted from the centre. Those migrants that could not or did not want to be deported to their country of origin were put on the street, without any right to shelter or care.

The Ter Apel eviction is part of a larger phenomenon. Great numbers of undocumented refugees are currently living outside of the Dutch system. Approximately 40,000 people are systematically held in administrative detention for up to eighteen months—and this process can be repeated endlessly. In this way, Dutch bureaucracy has created a substantial infringement on migrant human rights and dignity. Affected refugees depend on the charity and good will of private people and struggle for their livelihoods.

Tens of thousands of refugees essentially disappear into the fringes of Dutch society. They tend to live their undocumented lives hidden away from the system. But more and more of them refuse to hide. Instead, they fight for life and hope. "We are here," the evicted refugees in Ter Apel said collectively. And in order to add power to their statement, they built up a tented camp right in front of the centre from which they were sent away. With their slogan, the refugees express that they too are human beings, they have nowhere to go, and they will be around until a solution respectful of their human rights is found.

A meeting place of public manifestation
The initial tented camp outside of the refugee centre in Ter Apel was soon moved to the Amsterdam neighbourhood of Osdorp. Here, a growing number of refugees found shelter, food, safety, and medical care. Soon, the Osdorp camp became a place of public manifestation, a stage for direct and mediated exchange with neighbours and society at large. Around the camp, a network of helpers gathered to provide direct aid, temporary solutions and advice on more structural and political tactics.

Quite a few of the active supporters were artists, architects, and designers. They shared their design thinking and crafting skills with the inhabitants of the Osdorp camp, by way of facil-

← *We Are Here* is the slogan of the refugees-on-the-street. A map marks where the refugees are now and where they came from. The map is part of World Wide Nieuw-West, an art project by Marjolijn Boterenbrood. The project focuses on the global connections of people and businesses in an Amsterdam suburb.
Design: Marjolijn Boterenbrood

itating *Design the Future* workshops. Additionally, Migrant to Migrant (M2M) Radio hosted a conference that elaborated on the organisational structure of the group of refugees. If they were to inform the public, maintain communication between the different refugee groups, and take care of the overall day-to-day organisation of the camp, some form of representation was required.

Self-organisation:
the Parliament of Refugees

This is how the idea of the *Parliament of Refugees* was born. The parliament is a representative body that articulates the points of view of the various refugee groups, finds the common ground between them, and moulds this into a coherent discourse that can then be used to enter into a dialogue with the authorities and Dutch society. Consequently, the existence of the camp and its inhabitants quickly became known to the Dutch public. Through demonstrations and actions as well as by their presence in the media and in politics, the refugees powerfully joined the public and political debate.

Theatre of Hope:
refugees creating their own country

Through the design workshops that were offered by volunteer designers, the concept of the *Theatre of Hope* was born: the refugees were to create a stage for dialogue with mainstream Dutch society in search of a normal life. The *Theatre of Hope* project is meant to meet the two most urgent needs of the refugees: it is to offer a safe and warm place to stay as well as a space to develop their movement. An involved migration professor interprets it as the refugees "creating their own country."

After the camp in Osdorp was evicted, a church was squatted. With the help of architects and other supporters, over one hundred refugees have created another temporary place to live together here. They continue to build a support system around them that is based on public manifestation. The demonstrative "camp" attracts wide media exposure and negotiations with counsellors, mayors, ministers, members of parliament, and diplomats are ongoing. General meetings bring all campers together and a public General Assembly ratifies the steps proposed. Public actions at the offices of the Immigration Service and in front of the Parliament are all public performances of presence, passion, and the power to unite.

↓ Chekh El Mouthena Marrakchy (refugee from Mauritania) and Cheikh 'Papa' Sakho (neighbour and former refugee from Senegal) of M2M Radio painted the symbol for *We Are Here* that says: "Have a big eye to see, open your heart and reach out your hand to help us."
Photo: Willem van de Ven

↑ Refugees are experts when it comes to dealing with difficult situations. Artist Teun Castelein helps them to open a shop in the streets to offer their skills and advice to those in need. *Design: Teun Castelein*

↑ Amsterdam pop podium Paradiso staged We Are Here, a band of refugees led by front man Ciraque from Ivory Coast. Together with singer and songwriter Laurens Joensen, We Are Here was the support act for the Malian singer Salif Keita. *Photo: Jan-Dirk van den Burg*

Instead of counting on the support of the relevant authorities, the refugees will continue to depend on the goodwill and support from the public at large. This is ultimately what the *Theatre of Hope* is all about: it is about engaging the public in such a way that it feels connected to the refugees' cause. Rather than leaving the branding of the initiative up to the mainstream media, designers have been mobilised to help to create space for imagination, self-representation, and true connection with supporters and

the public at large. It is here, that the refugees find starting points for their renewed livelihoods. The *Theatre of Hope* represents a public space where supporters and refugees meet and create together. Essentially, it is about embedding the concepts of democracy and solidarity with new meaning. After the refugees leave the church —their eviction from the church is expected in the spring of 2013—they will essentially take the *Theatre of Hope* along on their journey. Wherever they may go next.

SUSTAINIST DESIGN FEATURES

The design of the We Are Here initiative is essentially about building relationships between refugees and mainstream Dutch society. The related design question —which might be called sustainist—focuses on how a "commons" can be created where the general public can offer support and engage with the cause of the refugees. Additionally, it functions as a "space" in which the refugees can develop their movement. Their overall aim is to express their message in a powerful way and channel the public debate.

→ The Theatre of Hope results from a collaborative design process in which the refugees took

the lead as much as possible. It shows that building relationships and mutual trust takes time, but is key to effective co-creation.

→ We Are Here is a manifestation of the need for the design of situations that facilitate resilience when formal institutions take a step back.

→ By making places that are accessible to the public and the media, the refugees are able to connect to people that can help on various levels: from providing food to legal advice. Results of the co-design workshops are physical and mental stepping stones for the future, however insecure it may be.

● LOCALISM

The call "We are here" says it all: the refugees belong just where they are. The refugees raise awareness of the fact that we live in a world of interconnected local worlds. Bringing this fusion of local qualities into the design process supplements the way in which we look at place-making and community building.

● CONNECTEDNESS

Designing for connectedness concerns various aspects, from empathy and understanding to connecting the public to a cause. Designing events to celebrate togetherness and collaborative action

is a way to encourage supporters to join in and become part of the network.

● PROPORTIONALITY

Small steps in the design process take into account the individual problems as well as the potential of the refugees, but also of their neighbours and other helpers.

Architectural activism

Making the city of Rotterdam together

Luchtsingel is a crowd funded urban design project that aims to reconnect the currently isolated and run-down Rotterdam neighbourhood of Hofbogen by building a 350-meter pedestrian bridge that will reconnect it to the central district of the city. Luchtsingel literally translates into "canal of air." It is used as a metaphor to refer to the comparable structure of the traditional Dutch city canals—except that Luchtsingel will be lifted up into the air, and will not be filled with water but with pedestrians instead.

Luchtsingel was initiated by the architects of Zones Urbaines Sensibles (ZUS). ZUS is of the opinion that architecture has become marginalised in the last two decades by responding primarily to market demands rather than public needs. That's why it wants to reemphasise architecture's important public function. Starting from the belief that everything and every place has the inherent potential to be unique and exciting, ZUS investigates the urban landscape in an attempt to expose contemporary social challenges. Ranging from urban plans and architecture to installations and fashion, it offers solicited and unsolicited advice and design that is inspired by the specific qualities of the context and that is meant to encourage intervention in the current state of things.

Luchtsingel is set within the broader context of I Make Rotterdam, an initiative by the International Architecture Biennale Rotterdam (IABR) and ZUS, that focuses on new ways of creating urban quality of life in a post-crisis economy. I Make Rotterdam (2012-2014) is meant to offer a contemporary alternative to the traditional practice of large-scale city planning. Within the context of the I make Rotterdam initiative, different projects were initiated by different parties. Luchtsingel is one of them and forms the backbone of the initiative as it ties the different projects together.

A successful formula: building Luchtsingel together

In less than a year, Luchtsingel went from initiation to realisation. It is a fully crowd funded project that anyone can contribute to. This alternative way of fund raising has proven to be a successful formula for Luchtsingel. More than 1,300 people have contributed to

← The city centre of Rotterdam by night showing the Luchtsingel, a pedestrian bridge over a busy traffic junction. *Photo: Ossip van Duivenbode*

the bridge by buying the wooden boards that are used in the construction of the bridge. The boards are personalised by adding the name, message or wedding date of the person that paid for it.

Luchtsingel is being built in different phases. The first part of the bridge was built in 2012. Next, the bridge will be extended by another one hundred meters in the direction of the neighbourhood of Hofbogen in June 2013. By phasing the building process, the actual Luchtsingel becomes visible step by step, which allows for people to become involved and anticipate the effects of the end product.

Urban life up in the air

Luchtsingel aims to revive urban quality of life by designing small-scale interventions to interact with life in the city. For example, the area surrounding the adjoining Hofplein is currently considered to be at the backside of the city of Rotterdam. Cars dominate it and there is a lack of public space at street level. The number of empty buildings is increasing quickly. With the development of Luchtsingel, combined with other initiatives and developments at street level, the area will gain safe and green public space, which will make the area attractive and lively

again—in addition to offering new access to it. In the slipstream of Luchtsingel, many other initiatives have followed. For example, a cultural square (Cultuurplein) is in the making and will be built early 2014. Cultuurplein, a new commons, is a place where cultural activities can take place in a green setting on a rooftop in Hofbogen area, right where Luchtsingel will be landing. Also, Biergarten—one of the sunniest terraces in the city of Rotterdam—was established and enjoyed by a great number of Rotterdammers. Additionally, Dakakker was initiated, which is a rooftop that is wholly dedicated to urban farming.

Unsolicited advice

ZUS came up with the idea for Luchtsingel while looking into the city of Rotterdam's central district master plan. The master plan contains the redesign of the street plan in the Hofbogen area to accommodate redevelopments that are planned for the city centre. The pedestrian bridge connecting the centre with Hofbogen turns out to be a perfectly logical addition to the city's plans. ZUS was not asked to contribute its thoughts but, rather, took its own initiative—a manifestation of architectural activism with much desired social impact.

↑ An artist impression showing the 350-meter pedestrian bridge, which will reconnect the city centre of Rotterdam to the Hofbogen area. Luchtsingel is the first step in returning urban quality of life to the area by adding small-scale interventions to the urban fabric. *Source: ZUS*

↑ The Luchtsingel enters an empty office building that is currently being redeveloped as a temporary hotspot for creative businesses. *Photo: Ossip van Duivenbode*

↑ Luchtsingel in the making.
Photo: Ossip van Duivenbode

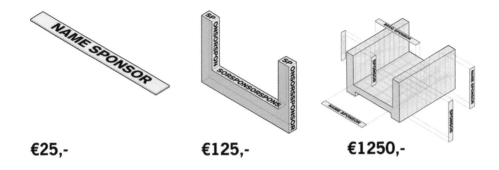

€25,-   **€125,-**   **€1250,-**

↑ One of the primary
→ driving forces of
crowd funded urbanism
is implementing projects
that do not easily attract
government funding, but
that are interesting to the
audience nonetheless.
In the example of Lucht-
singel, each contributor
invests in a plank with his
or her name on it. *Source:
ZUS / Photo: Ossip van
Duivenbode*

← Luchtsingel is a fully
crowd funded project:
anyone can contribute.
Photo: Design Art News

Luchtsingel and the initiatives related to it bring different sustainist elements together. Jointly, they connect social and ecological sustainability. They are about pro-actively involving citizens in reviving urban green and creating new common ground. The design approach is collaborative, contextual, and activist.

● SHARING

Crowd funding not only provides an alternative way of fund raising but, by personalising the wooden boards, it will remain a long lasting physical landmark of a "sharing culture."

● LOCALISM

ZUS was inspired by the specific qualities of the Hofbogen area to create localist attributes with their "canal of air," such as a new sense of place and locally rooted experiences. The project gives meaning to newly created public space and to a new commons.

● CONNECTEDNESS

The bridge reconnects pedestrians to a local neighbourhood that was previously dominated by cars. The project is about redesigning the relationship that people have with the urban environment and with each other. Luchtsingel is building a community where there wasn't one before.

↑ Photo: Design Art News

Leapfrogging scarcity

A civilisation starter kit in the making

The **Global Village Construction Set** (GVCS) is an open source technological platform that unites farmers, engineers, and others. Together, they prototype the fifty industrial machines that are needed to build a small, sustainable civilisation that accommodates modern comforts. Included are machines such as tractors, bakery ovens, dairy milkers, and cars. All machines are intended to be modular, do-it-yourself, and low-cost. In this way, the Global Village Construction Set is much like a life-size Lego set that has the potential to create entire economies. Groups in different parts of the United States are developing blueprints that are then built and tested at a farm in rural Missouri. It is the team's mission to ultimately be able to offer clear-cut fabrication instructions to help communities become more self-sufficient.
The entire set of fifty machines is scheduled for release late 2015.

← The Global Village Construction Set (GVCS) team with founder Marcin Jakubowski in the middle.
Photo: Open Source Ecology

↑ LifeTrac is a low-cost, multi-purpose open source tractor. It serves as a workhorse backbone for many GVCS technologies. The machine is built with a focus on lifetime design and ease of repair. Four hydraulic motors provide steer power to the wheels. A chain tread system enables navigation of extreme terrain. *Photo: Open Source Ecology*

Physicist Marcin Jakubowski founded the initiative in 2003 when his industrially manufactured tractor kept breaking down. This motivated him to look into robust yet low-cost machines that he could build himself. His efforts were rewarded as he discovered that it is indeed possible to achieve industrial productivity on a small scale. When he started sharing his designs online via the Open Source Ecology Wiki, people from all over the world began prototyping new machines. A movement was born.

An entirely new open business model

The popularity of the project demonstrates that the open-source methodology can be effective far beyond the world of software development. It has now claimed its rightful place in the world of hardware, too. Jakubowski firmly focuses on hardware, because he is certain it can change people's lives in tangible and material ways. And the results so far are quite convincing. On average, the costs of building and maintaining the GVCS machines are about eight times lower as compared to buying similar machines from industrial manufacturers. This significantly lowers the barriers for newcomers to enter into farming, building, and manufacturing. It creates opportunities for an entirely new open business model—not just for people in the West, but in the developing world alike.

In January 2013, the Global Village Construction Set was presented in Haiti as part of the *Relief 2.0 Panel on Sustainable Recovery* that aims to contribute to the recovery efforts since the major earthquake in 2010. There is particular potential here for use of the *Life Trac*, which is a multi-purpose tractor that doubles as a workhorse backbone for many of the other GVCS machines. Also, the *Power Cube* —a universal, self-contained power unit that is designed to be an interchangeable power supply for GVCS technologies—could prove to be very useful in this context. Both of them will be used as pilots for local production.

↑ A late-night show starring the GVCS LifeTrac open source tractor.

↑ The Liberator is an automatic press for compressed earth bricks. High in throughput—it is able to produce up to 16 bricks per minute—it is named The Liberator because it is intended to free people from the single highest cost of living: housing. *Photo: Open Source Ecology*

Cultural transformation is on its way

The culturally transformative potential of this and other open hardware technology projects is vast. In the decades to come, the associated do-it-yourself culture will be an important asset in fighting the scarcity that the world currently experiences. In this light, Jakubowski emphasises the artificiality of the current scarcity. Instead, he advocates the idea of an era of "post-scarcity." He says: "The scarcity-based economy is the status quo of today because of the way human relations have evolved. Not everybody is provided for. There is a lot of suffering in an absolute abundance of resources, such as rocks, sunlight, plants, and water, from which all economic wealth originates. (…) Post-scarcity means that we would be connected more closely to [those] resources, when we have the means and tools to transform those resources into the feedstock of modern civilisation."

→ OPENSOURCEECOLOGY.ORG

→ OPENSOURCEECOLOGY.ORG/WIKI/
GLOBAL_VILLAGE_CONSTRUCTION_SET

→ BLOG.OPENSOURCEECOLOGY.ORG/2013/01/
MACHINE-DEPLOYMENT-AND-PILOT-PROJECTS

The Global Village Construction Set embraces sustainist culture by practising an open network approach and emphasising nature as a source. The open hardware technological platform enables communities to build and use robust and low-cost machines, creating opportunities for an open business model with new players. The initiative (re)connects people to the abundant natural resources and their potential.

● SHARING

By sharing his designs, the founder of GVCS has created an open source ecology Wiki as well as a new movement. The sharing of knowledge for building open source hardware can help to unleash massive amounts of human potential and can change people's lives significantly.

● PROPORTIONALITY

Small-scale and sustainable initiatives like GVCS emphasise the fact that the scarcity-based economy we have created is partly artificial and unnecessary. When specific knowledge and materials are used to make what is needed in the right place at the right time, scarcity will no longer rule the economic system.

The Global Village Construction Set

↑ An overview of the available designs for various sorts of tools, ranging from a concrete mixer to a bulldozer, a laser cutter to a bakery oven, and a sawmill to a dairy milking machine—they are all envisioned to be part of the Civilisation Starter Kit. *Source: Open Source Ecology*

Game design in aid of medical science

Curing protein-related diseases competitively and collaboratively

In 2008, scientists at the University of Washington released a game called **Foldit** that enables ordinary gamers to contribute to scientific research. They are hoping that a critical mass of gamers will embrace the game and, in the process, will significantly help their medical research. "Already, some 60,000 people worldwide have taken on the challenge," principal investigator Zoran Popovic says. He hopes that Foldit's initial results will convince sceptics that scientific discovery games can actually lead to important and real breakthroughs in the world of science.

Foldit indirectly challenges gamers to predict and design the structures of proteins in the hopes of better understanding how they work and why they might be causing trouble in the human body. "With all the things proteins do to keep our bodies functioning and healthy, they can be involved in disease in many different ways. The more we know about [them], the better new proteins we can design to combat the disease-related proteins and cure the diseases," project lead Seth Cooper explains.

Playing Tetris to advance biochemistry

Foldit attempts to predict the structure of a protein by taking advantage of humans' puzzle-solving intuitions and has people play competi-tively to fold the best proteins. "The approach we have taken is to combine the spatial reasoning and problem solving of people with the number-crunching optimisation power of computers," Popovic adds. Thousands of people around the world have played Foldit already—a game much like the tile-matching puzzle video game Tetris —to help biochemists to tackle protein-related questions.

Remarkably, few of the gamers that are now actively involved have a background in bio-chemistry. Yet still, they are working to design brand new proteins that could help prevent or treat diseases such as HIV/AIDS, cancer, and the flu. "There are all kinds of players of different professions, ages, and nationalities."

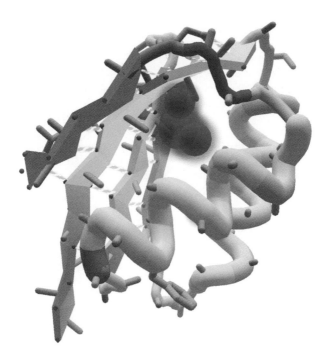

↑ The online game Foldit is designed to reveal the shortcuts that are used by nature to weave a tangle of amino acids, like the one shown here, into a protein. Players move pieces around until they fit. Every piece that is moved affects every other piece on the board. *Source: The University of Washington*

↓ A player uses the "rebuild" tool to explore different backbones in a region of the protein. The transparent purple tube shows the backbone change that is being considered by the player. *Source: The University of Washington*

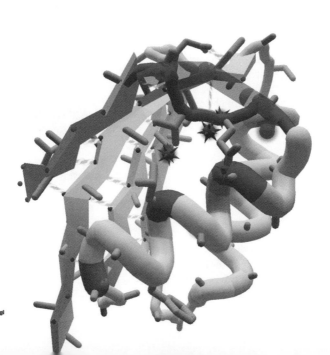

The fact that people can play the game together has proven to be a very important feature of the game. "Players can form groups and share the solutions that they have found. Players may have different skills, so by working together they may be able to find things that they wouldn't have found alone."

Protein folding by mass collaboration and creativity

The game helps scientists to gain insight into the "behaviour" of proteins. "Proteins are the workhorses in every cell of every living thing," Cooper explains. "Your body is made up of trillions of cells, of all different kinds: muscle cells, brain cells, blood cells, and more. Inside those cells, proteins are allowing your body to do what it does: break down food to power your muscles, send signals through your brain that control the body, and transport nutrients through your blood." When proteins stop working properly, disease occurs.

Essentially, a protein is made up of a long chain of amino acids. To make a protein, the amino acids form an unbranched chain, much like a line of people holding hands. Depending on the specific make-up of the protein, the chain folds up into a very specific shape—the same shape every time. "Most proteins do this all by themselves, although some need extra help to fold into the right shape. The unique shape of a particular protein is the most stable state it can adopt."

While gaming, research groups take the lead and define sub-challenges with specific goals and frameworks, carrying names like *675: Hydrogen-producing Catalyst Dimer*. Players can be individuals or groups, such as *l'Alliance Francophone*, *Team Hungary* and *Void Crushers*. Introductory levels teach the rules, which are the same laws of physics by which protein strands curl and twist into three-dimensional shapes. These are key to solving biological mysteries ranging from Alzheimer's to vaccines.

Teaching human strategies to computers

The number of different ways in which a protein can fold is astronomical, because there are so many degrees of freedom. Figuring out which of the many possible structures is the best one is considered one of the hardest problems in biology today. Foldit accommodates this problem: "We've already found that for certain types of

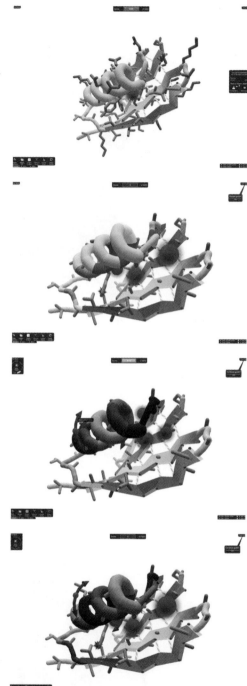

↑ A player uses the "tweak" tool to rotate a helix on the protein. The purple arrows allow the player to control the rotation. *Source: The University of Washington*

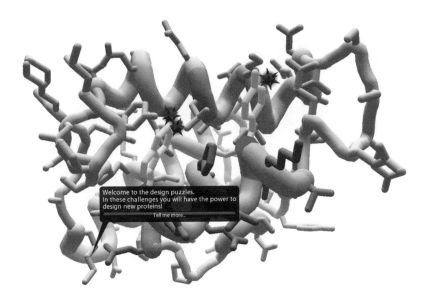

Welcome to the design puzzles.
In these challenges you will have the power to design new proteins!
Tell me more...

Pull Mode　　Design Mode

↑ A player starts an introductory level on protein design. Text bubble hints will introduce the basic concepts of protein design and help guide the player to the level's solution. *Source: The University of Washington*

structural rearrangement of partially folded proteins, players were often able to find better solutions than purely algorithmic approaches. Players were also able to resolve the structure of a virus protein that had remained unsolved by any experimental or computational method. Experimentalists had been working on it for over ten years." Foldit uses the newly acquired knowledge to start teaching human strategies to computers, so that they will ultimately fold proteins faster than ever before.

⊸ NEWS.CNET.COM

⊸ FOLD.IT

SUSTAINIST DESIGN FEATURES

Foldit qualifies as sustainist design, because it manifests the shift towards a networked and "pro-am" design process. Foldit was designed as an open gaming platform that mobilises playful mass collaboration and mass creativity to strengthen medical research.

→ The human-centred, accessible game design allows people with different expertise and skill sets to work together. Experts and non-experts can make equally useful contributions.

→ Foldit uses the power of gaming technology to make humans' puzzle solving skills valuable for medical science.

● SHARING

Foldit makes use of the power of open exchange. The game essentially creates a shared space— a new commons, if you will—where people can collaborate, play together, share their findings, and learn from one another.

● CONNECTEDNESS

The game offers a space for community building where various people can connect with medical scientist for the sake of curing, often life-threatening, protein-related diseases.

Pigs as designers

Gaming to improve wellbeing

Pig Chase is a game that targets both pigs and humans—as players. The game's primary aim is to use play to transform the way we relate to domesticated pigs. It does so by triggering new forms of human-pig interaction. By speaking to both the human and animal player's cognitive abilities, opportunities are created for the forging of new relationships that would ideally benefit both the human and animal player.

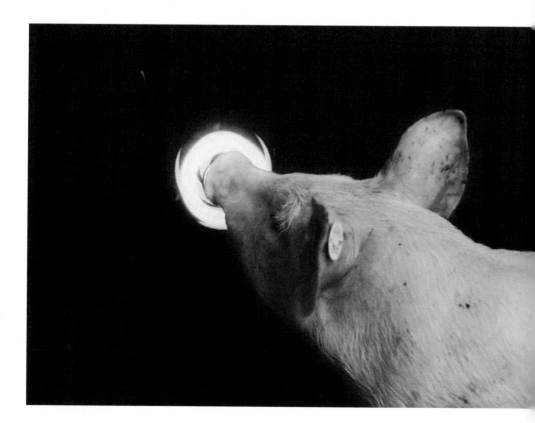

← Pigs play the game with the help of a large display that is sensitive to touch. A human-controlled ball of light moves around on the display. When the pig touches the ball, it fires colourful sparks. *Photo: Hein Lagerweij*

↑ Humans play the game on a tablet computer such as an iPad. They move the ball of light with their finger and see the pigs' snouts as if they were on the other side of the screen. *Photo: Hein Lagerweij*

For several years, designers and researchers at the Utrecht School of the Arts (HKU) and Wageningen University and Research Centre (Wageningen UR) have been working on a computer game that enables pigs and people to interact and play together. The human player can control the projection of light on the pig-pen's wall via his iPad. It's the human player's goal to capture and retain the naturally curious pig's attention, so as to encourage the pig to move past a series of targets.

Pigs like play, too

It's not only people that like to play. Pigs do, too. Studies of pig cognition have shown pigs to have well-developed, large brains. In crowded conditions, pigs are prone to stress and boredom-related behaviour. Since 2001, European legislation has made it compulsory for pig farmers to provide entertainment in the pens to combat boredom, aggression, and tail biting amongst

pigs. In order to meet the regulations, farmers have been experimenting with simple toys such as balls, chains, and ropes. They are social, playful animals and their cognitive abilities make them capable of mastering simple computer games. In practice however, it proves to be difficult to provide the animals with an adequate challenge.

Over the past year, designers Kars Alfrink, Irene van Peer, and Hein Lagerweij (all affiliated with the HKU research group Creative Design for Playful Impact), philosopher Clemens Driessen of Wageningen University, and animal welfare specialist Marc Bracke of Wageningen UR Livestock Research rose to the challenge and have been working on a computer game for pigs. Their aim is two-fold: they want to fulfil the pig's need to play, and in the process, attempt to establish a different relationship between pigs and humans.

↗ The game Pig Chase involves an interactive display that is mounted on the pigpen's wall. The goal for both players is to collaborate effectively. This means that the pig's snout and the human's finger on the tablet computer should move towards the same goal at the same time. If successful, this triggers a colourful display of fireworks. An additional challenge for humans is to maintain contact with the pig's snout. If the human player fails to do so, his ball of light fizzles out. The game enables humans and pigs to connect and interact.
Photo: Hein Lagerweij

Co-designing with pigs

Pig farmers and their pigs have been closely involved in the design process. They have been helping to create the game by responding to different elements of the game throughout the test phase. As experimentation progressed, the designers found out that pigs are actually very interested in the light effects that accompany the video imagery and make an effort to follow the light with their snouts. This discovery inspired the current set-up of the game in which a human player controls the light effects, which will then capture the naturally curious pig's attention, who will be triggered to follow the light towards a series of targets.

→ The number of targets that a human and pig hit in one session is kept track of and shown in a high score table. *Photo: Hein Lagerweij*

Connecting humans and animals

In the process of prototyping, the project team continuously attempts to maximise the positive impact of the game on pig welfare. Although the real value of this type of "pig entertainment" is far from clear, Clemens Driessen's research focuses on ways in which the development of new technologies can be used to resolve some aspects of the societal debate on animal welfare. Moral views on animal welfare might change over time as a result of the effect that new technologies might have on farming styles and how we understand these. In the process, a computer game provides a playful way of finding out what is interesting entertainment for pigs and the role that people may play in this regard. The field of human and animal interaction by means of information technology is in its early stages worldwide, but it provides opportunities for forging relationships with animals in new ways, while learning new things about the cognitive capacities of both animals and people.

Pig Chase is being developed as a design research tool by the Utrecht School of the Arts and Wageningen University.

 PLAYINGWITHPIGS.NL

SUSTAINIST DESIGN EVOLUTION

—

The paths ahead:
let's bring sustainist
qualities into our
social designs

A first **exploration**

This guide offers an initial exploration of what sustainist design is and what it can become. Here we move our focus from where we are to where we may be going. We will reflect on where we have travelled so far and what we have seen. And we draw some **"lines in the sand"** to look forward and to open a discussion on the future development of sustainist design.

We have looked at the changing landscape of social design through our sustainist lens. Through a dozen insightful stories we revealed a wide-ranging practice of social and sustainable design. And now, in this final part of the book, we will bring things together again. Here, we will tease out **common threads**, review the **changing landscape**, and look ahead at the evolution of sustainist design.

We will chart our continuing journey in three stages. First, we will share **"field notes"** on our encounters with new practices and explore their relevance for social design. Second, we will summarise the defining features of sustainist design thinking and doing by introducing a number of **"guideposts."** And finally, we ask what we—and you, and all of us— will need to do to become **"sustainist designers."** We end by presenting some concluding observations, not as an endpoint or a destination, but rather as an open beginning for the further development of sustainist design.

→ MICHIEL SCHWARZ
& JOOST ELFFERS
authors of *Sustainism
is the New Modernism:
A Cultural Manifesto
for the Sustainist
Era*, 2010

"In sustainist world-making there is: no ecology without community, no development without equity, no design that is not co-designed, no value without shared meaning, no information that is not based on open source, no action without local consideration, no community without participation, no sustainability without fairness"

FIELD NOTES

—

Sustainist observations for a new social design agenda

Common threads:
transforming what designers do, why, and how

The new landscape of social design exposed by our twelve examples includes practices of social innovation and sustainable change that many traditional designers would not immediately classify as "design." What we have seen does indeed look like a new playing field, with different players, and new kinds of play. The cases illustrate that design for social innovation can come in very different forms. Yet, there are common threads and recurrent features that emerge from this diversity. We present some of our "field notes" below, thereby marking a number of emerging patterns and observations based on the social design practices that we have reviewed. These observations outline the changing field of social design and offer us some of the ingredients of a new social design agenda for the sustainist era.

The design cases in this guide display a great diversity. But the fact that we were able to bring them together under a single banner suggests that they are part of a wider cultural transformation. The first thing that our social design stories reflect is a common view of the world, underpinned by the conviction that design can be a positive force in social change. Each of the cases addresses a complex issue that requires more than "design as usual" to resolve it—much more in fact. It requires a radical new outlook on what design encompasses and how designers can affect change. The initiators of all twelve initiatives are triggered by their belief that things could and should be different. They are all closely involved with their cause—concerned with social innovation and sustainable change—and work from the heart as well as the head. What's more, they know they are not alone as they are collaborating with likeminded people and organisations that want to see a similar change in the world.

What comes into view is a new context in which designers are taking on new responsibilities. Designers are increasingly becoming social designers who wish to contribute to new forms of entrepreneurship and citizen initiatives that are making our environments more socially and ecologically sustainable. They offer their specific skills and expertise to address societal issues.

Reshaping the social design process

We can see how the focus on social innovation is transforming design practice, whether it's about designing interventions in the public domain, new forms of scientific research, or situations from which social and sustainable entrepreneurship can grow. Whilst qualities such as sharing and connecting inform the direction of design, we can see how the process of social design is changing too. It is increasingly incorporating sustainist values. Design is becoming co-design: it becomes open, collaborative, value-driven, and engaging.

All of our social design cases underscore the importance of process. Clearly, process and content are closely related. The new forms of social design that we have surveyed reveal a real change in approach that has as much to do with the questions of "how" and "with whom," as it is concerned with the overall purpose of the designs.

Notes from the field: emerging patterns in the design process

Our design examples illustrate how social design processes are being reshaped in the sustainist era. A number of patterns can be seen in the way social design is organised, who is included in the process, and how. We share some of our "notes from the field" below. They are brief observations on the changing process in design practice.

NOTE 1

SHARING OPENLY TOGETHER

P. 96 → 99

Sharing and creating together is the new business model, according to the makers of the **Global Village Construction Set** which uses an open source online platform for sharing instructions to build tools for small-scale production. If it were up to them, every local community would build its own machines in order to grow food, use its land, and become more self-sufficient that way. It illustrates what shared effort and open exchange may achieve: it creates accessibility, enables co-design with users, and facilitates production where and when it is needed. In the case

P. 100 → 103

of the **Foldit** game, the power of open sharing and collaborative development comes in the form of collaborative research, demonstrating how "winning by sharing" can fuel creativity.

SELF-ORGANISATION AND ENGAGEMENT

P. 72 → 77

P. 78 → 81

Taking matters in your own hands—both literally and metaphorically speaking—is a recurring pattern, too. In the case of **Agrocité**, the designers clearly show how the process of giving meaning to local engagement is a multi-dimensional story. It combines collective making, growing healthy food, reducing the human footprint, and community control over the production process and public space. Much like Agrocité, the case of **Lamon Luther** serves as an example of the power of civic engagement. It demonstrates how it is able to create work and quality of life cooperatively. These examples suggest that meaningful empowerment needs both bottom-up and top-down engagement, combined with the involvement of stakeholders. Both cases take embedded knowledge as the starting point of their design process, whilst much of the impetus comes from the passion of the participants.

NOTE 3 **BUILDING CROSSOVERS AND BRIDGING GAPS**

P. 68 → 71

P. 62 → 67
P. 86 → 89
P. 104 → 107
P. 90 → 95

Building crossovers between communities and bridging different kinds of knowledge can be a crucial ingredient to designing meaningful situations. Co-creation often requires connecting people from different social worlds and building mutual trust. This becomes visible in our cases in different forms. It is exposed by the direct contact between the designer and the local brewers in the **Outside Brewery** initiative. It also becomes visible by the crossovers that are built between the world of sports and public health in the case of **WASH United**, between undocumented refuges and the public in **We Are Here**, between humans and animals in **Pig Chase**, and between separated neighbourhoods in Rotterdam in the case of **Luchtsingel**. Designers can actively employ their skills where greater proximity and closer connection is required, be it cultural, emotional, or geographical.

NOTE 4 **CREATING HUBS AND COMMONS**

P. 72 → 77
P. 90 → 95

Places for connecting and exchanging play a central role in building creative communities that impact social design. Such social "hubs" are nodes in the network and often function as the kick-starter of innovative plans. This may involve physical shared work environments or "collaborative labs," as is the case in the projects of **Agrocité** and **Luchtsingel**. Those examples show how an undefined public space can be turned into a "shared space" or a "commons." Such commons become new forms of livelihoods, both as physical habitats and virtual shared spaces. Luchtsingel in particular makes visible how online hubs can empower real-life community building. It manifests itself as a meeting place in the physical city and is powered by an online platform for crowd funding.

NOTE 5

EMBRACING THE POSITIVE VALUE OF LIMITS

P. 82 → 85

P. 78 → 81

Many of the new initiatives and movements we have looked at are small-scale by design, as well as local. In such forms of social design we recognise the positive value of limit, in scale and aspiration. To impose limits becomes a necessary condition for the essential qualities of the design project. The story of **Rural Spark** shows how small-scale can have real advantages over large systems design. Rural Spark combines small-scale energy production with the encouragement of local entrepreneurship to take responsibility for its distribution. Its "smart grid" might even be less vulnerable than the current centralised energy grids. The craftsmanship of **Lamon Luther** makes visible how small-scale can contribute to meaningful relationships at the local level. The cooperative mode of crafts production reflects fundamentally different values. It rejects the mass production model, whilst benefiting the local community and encouraging responsibility.

NOTE 6

NEW WAYS OF LEARNING

P. 72 → 77

P. 62 → 67

The **Agrocité** programme in the Parisian suburb of Colombes demonstrates how urban locals have the potential to become educated urban farmers through small-scale workshops. Here we see new forms of learning based on peer-to-peer principles that promote learning from professionals and from each other. Playful collaboration, including rituals and drama, can be a strategy for learning within social design, as the **WASH United** case clearly shows. It can challenge players to explore new fields and learn about unknown worlds. Interactive media and computer games, as social platforms for sharing knowledge, enhance the design process.

NOTE 7

MEDIA AS A SOCIAL STRATEGY

P. 62 → 67

P. 58 → 61

WASH United places the power of media at the centre its strategy. The football-related visual rhetoric of its branding is causing the growing popularity of its events that are designed to bond people for the sake of improving hygiene. Media can be both a context and an ingredient in social design processes. "Media ecology" affects design for social innovation, as is well illustrated by the abundant public attention that the **Mine Kafon** is receiving. The visually attractive dandelion-like shape of the deminer and the mediagenic character of the designer's story are key elements in its public impact. Given the power and ubiquitous presence of media and social media, it is not surprising that these play a significant role in giving meaning to our social designs.

NOTE 8

NEW ROLES, NEW LEADERSHIP

P. 86 → 89

P. 52 → 57

The roles social designers play shift, as they become equal participants in processes of co-design. As they become increasingly engaged in social situations, they are no longer the "authors" that they were in the past, but are increasingly turning to facilitating, curating and inspiring as their core business. Cases such as **We Are Here** make clear that a different kind of creative leadership is required in this context. Instead of claiming uniqueness and autonomy, the social designers involved take responsibility for creating environments where the participants' creativity can flourish. In the case of **FairPhone**, design lead Bas van Abel is setting an example of a type of social design leadership that is more ambitious and vigorous with aspirations to force breakthroughs in complex design situations.

NOTE 9

FORMS OF DESIGN ACTIVISM

P. 52 → 57

P. 90 → 95

P. 96 → 99

The design cases we reviewed are concerned with social change. They are all to some extent geared towards actively changing established arrangements. We noticed how design processes inevitably have political dimensions and can become a form of "design activism," where designers' capabilities create openings for social and environmental change. The **FairPhone** case provides a powerful example. It clearly takes on the powers that govern mobile technology and challenges every step in the design process. It leads to a kind of social design that actively transfers power, away from dominant institutions, and empowers people to take control of their situation. In the case of the **Luchtsingel** project, the unsolicited design initiative of ZUS reflects an activist approach that both challenges established urban planning institutions and collaborates with them, setting an alternative agenda. The **Global Village Construction Set** takes it even one step further by aiming to make small businesses independent from an established system altogether.

GUIDEPOSTS

—

What are key features
in the emerging practice
of sustainist design?

From **social** design to **sustainist** design

A new generation of designers is encountering a whole new set of challenges on their journey. The essence of its novelty lies in the connection between social design and sustainable innovation. Our sustainist "lens" does not only give us new "sightlines" for viewing social design as a value-driven cultural movement, it also provides us with lines for development—"guidelines"—for an emerging design practice that we have termed sustainist design. We now have some sense of where we should look and where we should travel. As we enter this new terrain, we will need guideposts to find our path towards sustainist design.

The sustainist perspective—as can be gauged from the cases in this guide—highlights some features of social design theory and practice that have emerged in the last decade or so. The growing attention for co-design and open collaboration as well as the rise in design thinking to address social issues are cases in point (as the first part of this guide observes). Equally, sustainist design concurs with more integrative and contextualised design approaches. Our notion of sustainist design clearly is not an entirely new kind of designing. Rather, it incorporates a number of recent developments in "design for social innovation" and design for sustainable life. It re-emphasises the direction in which social design has been going—and in our view will be going—whilst making visible that it is part of a broader and deeper cultural transition.

Key features of sustainist design

What we are observing in reviewing design for social innovation is a transition towards forms of "sustainist design" that can be recognised by an underlying shift in focus. We recognise a number of defining features that act as orientation points in this new territory. We have formulated six. Let's call them our "guideposts" for sustainist design (see opposite page).

These guideposts give us a sense of direction while we develop the agenda for sustainist design and position its emerging practice in relation to social design. In the six paragraphs that follow we summarise some of our journey so far and outline what we see as the paths ahead.

1 SUSTAINIST DESIGN MARKS A SHIFT FROM FUNCTIONALITY TO CREATING MEANING

2 SUSTAINIST DESIGN EMPLOYS THE SOCIAL POWER OF DESIGN THINKING

3 SUSTAINIST DESIGN CENTRES ON RELATIONSHIPS AND SITUATIONS

4 SUSTAINIST DESIGN INCORPORATES COLLABORATION AND SHARED CREATIVITY

5 SUSTAINIST DESIGN EMPOWERS THROUGH THE CULTURE OF MAKING

6 SUSTAINIST DESIGN TREATS SUSTAINABILITY AS SOCIAL CHANGE

SUSTAINIST DESIGN MARKS A SHIFT FROM FUNCTIONALITY TO **CREATING MEANING**

The sustainist perspective puts people centre stage. But more than what's often called "human-centred" design, it goes beyond the usual idea of user experience and functional approaches. At the heart of sustainist design processes—as is demonstrated by many of the cases in this guide—is a search to create meaning through design. Put differently: our focus on value-driven design shifts our perspective from functionality to meaning. Sustainist design explicitly focuses on designing for meaningful engagement.

The examples presented in this guide reflect that successful social design is able to address the complexity of real-life situations, taking into account the multi-layered relationships that shape their meaning. The cases we have reviewed can all be seen as emergent and transformative situations, underpinned by particular values, perceptions, and intentions of the participants. Giving meaning to local engagement is often a multi-dimensional story. Take the case of urban farming, which combines collective making, growing healthy food, reducing the human footprint, and community control over the production process and public space.

Creating meaning in social design is conceived here as an open process. Sustainist design builds on and invites a culture of involvement and engagement. At the centre are communities, taking shared responsibility for shaping the living environments of which they are a part. Sustainist qualities encourage design of open and accessible activities, peer-to-peer education, empowerment of people, and small-scale social and sustainable enterprises. Sustainist designs are often underpinned by the desire to recast living conditions, or even lifestyles. Sometimes the only route forward to is to leave old values behind and embrace new ones. Whether we are speaking of a collective of craftsmen or Indian villagers seeking local small-scale energy solutions, people succeed in redesigning their circumstances and giving new meaning to their daily lives and livelihoods, in both content and form.

SUSTAINIST DESIGN EMPLOYS THE SOCIAL POWER OF **DESIGN THINKING**

Sustainist design opens up the design process. It builds on the idea that forms of creative innovation can be achieved by designers and "non-designers" alike. A new, open and collaborative design practice is emerging where, as Charles Leadbeater has it, "more people than ever will be able to contribute to this unfolding shared culture." It is this "social power" of the new design ethic, that connects sustainist design to the growing practice of design thinking. By involving stakeholders directly in the design process, and by including social and sustainability values in the design briefs, design thinking becomes a driver for social design.

Design thinking in the sustainist mode provides an action perspective to social design. It capitalises on the growing awareness that in principle anyone—consumers, citizens, workers, entrepreneurs, and amateurs—can contribute valuable knowledge and skills in the design processes. The idea of co-design is gaining ground, as people increasingly want to play their part in social design. Not just to be involved in designing their living environment, but also because they wish to actively influence their livelihoods.

Sustainist design takes this aboard and, in the process, changes the role of designers as we understood it in the modernist era. In the words of John Thackara: "In this new era of collaborative innovation, designers are having to evolve from being the individual authors of objects, or buildings, to being the facilitators of change among large groups of people." In the sustainist era, the significance of design thinking lies in its social dimensions. Sensitivity to context and the social connections implied by a design are key features of what Thackara has called "the transition from mindless development to design mindfulness." By bringing social sustainability values into the equation, design thinking becomes an explicitly social and ethical challenge.

 ## SUSTAINIST DESIGN CENTRES ON **RELATIONSHIPS** AND **SITUATIONS**

Sustainist approaches to social design focus on designing for relationships and connections. Relationships are at the very heart of our culture. As our social worlds are becoming increasingly part of a network society, designers are challenged to connect the nodes and to design what's going on between them. Dutch philosopher Henk Oosterling calls it "relational design." Designing the connections—a kind of "interface design"—is central to sustainist design: connections between places and communities, between services and their users, between media and citizens, between the land and consumers of food.

Sustainist design invites an altogether integrative approach that not only shapes interrelationships, but also acknowledges that designing the relevant context is inherent to the design challenge. The places we inhabit are never experienced as "islands" separated from their surroundings, and it is context that gives them meaning. Designing a place to live, for example in the case of the "refugee church" in the Netherlands, implies more than shelter in and of itself. The challenge is to make social relations an inherent part of the design of their new home. Designing conditions and circumstances collaboratively, and in an open process makes people part of the process of designing solutions. Involvement in collectively making the circumstances is key. It is this shaping of the social situation that defines the design challenge. As John Thackara has so aptly phrased it: "design *is* the situation."

This means that sustainist design takes a centred approach to situations. Co-designing in and with a community—be it a neighbourhood organisation, a user community, or a citizen group—requires taking a position that is as close as possible to the centre of a situation. We interact with our environments, but are also part of them. It suggests a kind of situated design approach that is integrative and that is developed from the inside out, rather than imposed from the outside. Not design *for* people, but rather creating situations that are conducive for collaboration are at the heart of new sustainist design processes.

 ## SUSTAINIST DESIGN INCORPORATES **COLLABORATION** AND **SHARED CREATIVITY**

Collaboration, open exchange and shared creativity are premises for sustainist design. They represent a new mentality where sharing and collaboration become key qualities at the heart of value-driven design processes. Sharing knowledge, information and creative resources opens paths towards design outcomes that are both socially and ecologically sustainable. Sustainist design strategies are design strategies that put a number of social attributes at their very core: collaborative, collective, inclusive, and shared. Sustainist design can thrive because of the social emergence of "We-Think" and "mass creativity," as Charles Leadbeater has called it.

Collaborative design and shared creativity are becoming the hallmarks of social design in a networked culture, where we no longer have to depend solely on expert-led, top-down approaches to addressing design challenges. Thanks partly to open social media and online platforms, "peer networks" are opening immense new opportunities for designing solutions based on collaboration, community, and shared resources. It will be "peer progressives" who hold the key to social change, Steven Johnson argues his book *Future Perfect: The Case for Progress in a Networked Age.* We view such developments as part of a movement towards sustainist design.

The Global Village Construction Set is a case of what Steven Johnson characterises as "No one in charge, but everyone." The design concept centres on open source collaborative development. It involves online networks but at least as important in its successful design, is the ability to produce locally and the will to share information and creative resources. It is precisely those kinds of connections between networks of technologies, intentions and human aspirations that offer new directions for sustainable and social design.

5 SUSTAINIST DESIGN EMPOWERS THROUGH THE **CULTURE OF MAKING**

With its emphasis on building connections, sustainist design (re)connects with a culture of making that can be seen in recent social design practices. The act of making and craftsmanship are witnessing a social resurgence. Sustainist design values the idea that "making is connecting," to cite the title of the book by David Gauntlett. As he observes: "Through making things and sharing them with the world, we increase our engagement with our social and physical environments."

The growing interest in making and the current re-emergence of a "skills culture" is a feature of change that is happening in design, and elsewhere. We view it as part of a move towards a sustainist design philosophy. To make is to think with your hands, says Richard Sennett in his book *The Craftsman* (2008), and it has much to do with the sustainist world of relationships. Craftsmanship is a value and a quality that is shaped through the exchange of knowledge and skills, through the relationships we have with our tools, materials and their origins, and through our awareness of the meaning we are adding by making.

The worldwide surge in do-it-yourself initiatives, as manifested in the Etsy platform, can be seen as part of the emerging sustainist culture. To make things ourselves becomes a kind of personal design strategy. We can either buy a product or service about which we have no inside knowledge, or we can make it ourselves. To find out how things are made, and to be able to take matters in your own hands literally, is becoming part of the sustainist design process. As Van Abel explains the design philosophy behind his FairPhone project: "If you can't open it, you don't own it."

Making can be a significant ingredient of strategies for co-design in the era of sustainism. It implies tapping into the (often hidden) talents of people—professionals and amateurs—as part of the new mentality of open exchange, sharing, and collaboration. It is an important part of designing for social innovation.

6 SUSTAINIST DESIGN TREATS SUSTAINABILITY AS SOCIAL CHANGE

At the heart of the sustainist design perspective is the idea that designing for sustainability will ultimately rest on social and cultural changes, as much as environmental concerns. Sustainist design is not a form of eco-design, rather it takes sustainability as including social, economic, and ethical dimensions. In our discourse, too—in the design world and elsewhere—we need to move beyond "green" to express a more encompassing notion of sustainability. Some innovators, such as Adam Werbach and Gunter Pauli, have suggested we call it "blue" instead. Whatever its colour, a central feature of sustainist design is that it takes an integrated social view of shaping sustainable life. In this Guide, FairPhone has given us a striking example of how environmental and social sustainability go together, and cannot be divorced from their ethical and political dimensions.

In the domain of social design it would be an important improvement if we would begin to view sustainability not merely as environmental progress, but in terms of social change. From a sustainist perspective, ecological matters should not be treated as separate items in our design briefs, but as part of a social and cultural sustainability agenda. In this guide, we have not singled out ecological design solutions, because we view them as part-and-parcel of more integrated design strategies. Concern for ecological impacts is itself a key social value in the sustainist era, connecting to other values (such as our four sustainist design qualities).

Sustainist design reconceptualises how we relate to nature and the natural environment, precisely because it sees it as a relationship—and we, people, co-design that relationship. "Nature changes along with us," says Koert van Mensvoort in his cultural project Next Nature. An example would be how changes in our food culture alter our relationships to land, nature, and animals. In a sustainist perspective, the relationships we have with nature become part of our value-driven social design agenda. The design of our natural environment thus inevitably becomes part of our social design strategy, not something that is part of another agenda. Put differently: "eco-design" as part of "socio-design."

MOVING FORWARD

—

What do we need to do to become sustainist designers?

From sustainist design thinking to **sustainist design practice**

Where do we go from here? Clearly our map is still rough. We have only begun charting some of the new field that is emerging. In previous times, we would simply turn our "guideposts" into methods and procedures to make our designs more sustainist. But in the sustainist era there is no linear path to the future, no blueprints, and no standard recipes to follow. Yet, there is a path ahead. In the final section of this guide we put forward a set of essential ingredients that are needed if we want to become more sustainist designers. They do not take the shape of a "toolbox" in the conventional sense of the word. Rather, they are stepping stones that will help us to move forward on our journey from sustainist design thinking to sustainist design practice. Hence, our open-ended question: what do we need to do to become sustainist designers?

Turning values into **design qualities**

At the core of this guide is the idea that we are experiencing a cultural shift in the way we look at the world. What we are seeing is a veritable movement towards sustainist ways of living. Our thinking about what it takes to be a "sustainist designer" starts with acknowledging such a vision of the future. That in itself is a point of view. It has been our vantage point from the outset. It also provides a context for asking what designers should be doing in the new era. When we view sustainism as a new design ethos, it begs the question how we see our role in this movement towards a more sustainist world. And we need to think about what strategies we might follow to bring our social designs onto a sustainist path.

Changing values have been central to this exploratory design guide. Our journey through the new domain has been inspired by the belief that social designers need to take note of how society has been turning to a different set of values. We have dwelled on the importance of value-driven design where social values, including sustainability, shape our design practices. Above all, we have focused on four core sustainist design qualities—sharing, localism, connectedness, and proportionality—and raised the challenge of how to bring these into our design briefs. Having journeyed through the new territory, we are even more convinced of the importance of this new sustainist agenda for social design. Now we need to turn sustainist design into practice. We view this as a collective challenge.

Sustainist design practice:
where, **what**, and **how**?

The sustainist design agenda recasts what we mean by "social design" and shifts our focus towards a new set of social attributes. The quality of our designs depends on the qualities we put into them. That's why we have translated sustainist values into design requirements. They are design qualities that create social value and drive the process of social design. Embracing such qualities is what makes us socially and ecologically responsible sustainist designers.

In moving social design onto a sustainist path, designers will need to concern themselves with three very basic questions:

1. **WHERE DO WE STAND?**
2. **WHAT DO WE WANT TO DO?**
3. **HOW DO WE DO IT?**

Here, at the very end of this guide, we put up for discussion a first set of elements. We associate them with what it means to be (or become) sustainist designers. Below, we structure them along the lines of the three questions we raise above.

1 ▶

WHERE DO WE STAND?

Getting involved in design for social change and design for sustainability means that we are taking position. It is a normative endeavour that implies a sense of responsibility in the role and position of the designer. It is characterised by:

√	A human-centred approach
√	A concern for social and ecological sustainability
√	A shift in focus towards meaning and purpose
√	Taking a stand, ethically and politically
√	Co-design with people and with nature
√	Design activism
√	Valuing the power of the commons
√	Considerations such as fairness

2 ▶

WHAT DO WE WANT TO DO?

This is the core of design for sustainist change. Embracing a value-driven design practice means connecting to the core qualities of sustainist culture. It is characterised by:

√ Designing for sustainable outcomes

√ Building on people's passions

√ Incorporating shareability

√ Valuing rootedness

√ Building relationships and communities

√ Strengthening local ties

√ Looking for the human scale

√ Choosing appropriate speed and size

√ Making open and inclusive designs

√ Creating fair livelihoods

3 ▶

HOW DO WE DO IT?

Sustainist design processes embrace values that enhance the sustainist movement. They support collective responsibility for addressing social and ecological issues, and provide the conditions for following a sustainist design agenda. They are characterised by:

√ Taking context into account

√ Focusing on place

√ Using the power of networks

√ Facilitating co-creation

√ Embracing participatory practices

√ Inspiring dialogues

√ Minimising ecological footprints

√ Incorporating local resources

√ Celebrating diversity

√ Searching out self-organising opportunities

√ Building trust with users and participants

√ Making it a learning experience

√ Using creative commons and open source

Join the **change**

This exploratory guide has tried to expose how there's a growing domain where design for social innovation and design for sustainability is coming together, and we have given it a name. We have put "sustainist design" on the map. Thus, we have made it part of a cultural movement by the name of "sustainism," which is growing worldwide. This is not as self-evident as it may seem, because the movement consists of millions of relatively small, local and grass-roots initiatives. Nonetheless, it is real and growing. Paul Hawken calls it "the largest movement in the world (…) that no one saw coming." Sustainist designers are not alone. They are part of this significant movement of change.

Sustainist design connects design for social innovation to sustainable innovation as well as the networked world. It takes social design firmly into the era of sustainism. Now we need to take it further and find out how it could shape our practice. Part of the challenge is to join forces by connecting initiatives and communities. To build on what others have already done, to hook up, to exchange experiences, to pool resources, and to build coalitions—it's all part of the sustainist ethic. Connecting the great diversity of rich examples under the single rubric of sustainist design can become empowering in itself.

This guide is a mere first exploration of the notion of sustainist design. It challenges all of us to include sustainist qualities into our future design briefs. And it challenges us to become "responsible designers," socially and ecologically. It raises more questions than it answers, but this may be a virtue: we view this guide not as an end point, but rather as a first stage in the development of a new domain of design thinking and design practice. We have shared our ideas and observations in the hope that they will be debated, developed, experimented with, and above all augmented and enhanced. We hope that they will inspire dialogues, connections, creations, as well as new initiatives.

You are what you **share**

This is not the end in another sense, too. Our exploration has not finished and, in a way, neither has this book. This guide is open-ended. In the same spirit as we started it, it is an open collaborative project that is ongoing and in many ways "work in progress." We set off with an open platform, opensustainistdesign.net, which then became our "research notebook" and a gathering place for ideas and sustainist design cases. We look forward to continuing the conversation. We extend an open invitation to contribute your ideas about what sustainist design is and what it could be. Share your thoughts on opensustainistdesign.net. Having put this *Sustainist Design Guide* on the table, let's explore what should be included in its 2.0 edition. Charting the further development of sustainist design is a collective challenge. We are making the future together. To be shared.

RESOURCES

—

References, authors
& acknowledgements

References & further reading

Bas van Abel, Lucas Evers, Roel Klaassen and Peter Troxler. *Open Design Now: Why design Cannot Remain Exclusive* (Amsterdam: BIS Publishers, 2011)

Wendell Berry. The Idea of a Local Economy, in: *Orion Magazine* (Winter 2001)

Wendell Berry. Compromise, Hell!, in: *Orion Magazine* (Nov/Dec 2004)

Eve Blossom. *Material Change: Design Thinking and the Social Entrepreneurship Movement* (New York: Metropolis Books, 2011)

Rachel Botsman and Roo Rogers. *What's Mine Is Yours: The rise of collaborative consumption* (New York: Harper, 2010)

Bristol Green Capital. *Bristol Inspiring Change* (Bristol: Alastair Sawday Publishing, 2011)

Tim Brown. *Change by Design: How design thinking transforms organizations and inspires innovation* (New York: Harper, 2009)

Tim Brown and Jocelyn Wyatt. Design Thinking for Social Innovation, in: *Stanford Social Innovation Review* (Winter 2010)

Beth Buczynski. *The Gen Y Guide to Collaborative Consumption*, in : Malcolm Harris with Neal Gorenflo (editors), *Share or Die: Voices of the get lost generation in the age of crisis* (New Society: Gabriola Island, 2012)

Center for a New American Dream. *Guide to Sharing: Exchanging stuff, time, skills and space*, published on newdream.org/programs/collaborative-communities/community-action-kit/sharing (Charlottesville: The Center for a New American Dream, 2013)

Etsy. *Hello Etsy: A Handbook on Small Business and Sustainability* (Berlin: Etsy Germany GmbH, 2011)

Alastair Fuad-Luke. *Design Activism: Beautiful strangeness for a sustainable world* (London: Earthscan, 2009)

Lisa Gansky. *The Mesh: Why the future of business is sharing* (New York: Portfolio/Penguin, 2010)

Kim Gaskins. In: Neal Gorenflo, The New Sharing Economy, on: shareable.net, 24 December 2010

David Gauntlett. *Making is connecting: The social meaning of creativity, from DIY and knitting to YouTube and Web 2.0* (Cambridge: Polity, 2011)

Paul Hawken. *Blessed Unrest: How the largest movement in the world came into being and why no one saw it coming* (New York: Penguin, 2007)

Paul Hawken. *Healing or Stealing? Commencement Address to the Class of 2009* (Portland: University of Portland, 3 May 2009)

Rob Hopkins. *The Transition Companion: Making your community more resilient in uncertain times* (Totnes Devon: Green Books, 2011)

François Jégou and Ezio Manzini. *Collaborative Services. Social innovation and design for sustainability* (Milan: Edizioni Polidesign, 2008)

Steven Johnson. *Future Perfect: The case for progress in a networked age* (London: Allen Lane, 2012)

Charles Leadbeater. *We-Think: The power of mass creativity* (London: Profile Books, 2008)

Charles Leadbeater. The Art of With, published on cornerhouse.org/art/art-media/the-art-of-with-essay (London: Cornerhouse, 2009)

Charles Leadbeater. *Cloud Culture: The future of global cultural relations* (London: Counterpoint, 2010)

Ezio Manzini. The new way of the future: Small, local, open and connected, in: *Social Space* (Singapore: Lien Centre for Social Innovation, Singapore Management University, 2011)

Bill McKibben. *Deep Economy: The wealth of communities and the durable future* (New York: Times Books, 2007)

Koert van Mensvoort and Hendrik-Jan Grievink (editors). *Next Nature: Nature changes along with us* (Barcelona: Actar, 2011)

Jeremy Millar and Michiel Schwarz. *Speed: Visions of an accelerated age* (London: Whitechapel Art Gallery/The Photographers' Gallery, 1998)

Robin Murray, Julie Caulier-Grice and Geoff Mulgan. *The Open Book of Social Innovation* (London: The Young Foundation/ NESTA, 2010)

OO:/NESTA. *Compendium for the Civic Economy: What our cities, towns and neighbourhoods should learn from 25 trailblazers* (Haarlem: Trancity*Valiz, revised in 2012)

Henk Oosterling. Dasein as Design / Or: Must Design Save the World? in: *From Mad Dutch Disease to Born to Adorn: Premsela Lectures 2004-2010* (Amsterdam: Premsela, Dutch Platform for Design and Fashion, 2010)

Gunter Pauli. *Blue Economy—10 Years, 100 Innovations, 100 Million Jobs* (Taos: Paradigm Publications, 2010)

Constantin Petou and Doina Petrescu / Atelier d'Architecture Autogerée. R-Urban Resilience, in: *ATLAS: Geography, Architecture and Change in an Interdependent World* (2012)

Marjetica Potrç. A Vision of the Future City and the Artist's Role as Mediator: Learning from Projects in Caracas and Amsterdam, published on design.hfbk-hamburg.de/index. php?page_id=138 (2012)

Woodcraft Saffron with Nicola Bacon, Lucia Caistor-Arender and Tricia Hackett. *Design for Social Sustainability: A framework for creating thriving new communities* (London: The Young Foundation, 2011)

Kirkpatrick Sale. *Human Scale* (New York: Coward, McCann & Geoghegan, 1980)

Juliet B. Schor. *Plenitude: The new economics of true wealth* (New York: Penguin, 2010)

E. F. Schumacher. *Small Is Beautiful: Economics as if people mattered* (London: Blond & Briggs, 1973)

Michiel Schwarz and Joost Elffers. *Sustainism is the New Modernism: A Cultural Manifesto for the Sustainist Era* (New York: DAP/Distributed Art Publishers, 2010)

Richard Sennett. *The Craftsman* (London: Penguin, 2009)

Richard Sennett. *Together: The rituals, pleasures and politics of cooperation* (New Haven & London: Yale, 2012)

Alex Steffen (editor). *World Changing: a user's guide for the 21st century* (New York: Abrams, 2006)

Woody Tasch. *Inquiries into the Nature of Slow Money: Investing as if food, farms, and fertility mattered* (Vermont: Chelsea Green, 2010)

John Thackara. *In the Bubble: Designing in a complex world* (Cambridge: MIT Press, 2005)

Authors

MICHIEL SCHWARZ

Michiel Schwarz is the co-creator (with designer Joost Elffers, 2010) of the cultural manifesto *Sustainism is the New Modernism* that provided the framework for this guide. His work as an independent cultural thinker, consultant and innovator has been concerned with how the future is shaped by culture. Over the last decades, he has initiated and developed cultural and policy-related projects on themes such as the network society, sustainable futures, digital media culture, creative innovation, and social design. He has instigated social debates, worked with creative lab Fabrica (Italy) and Design Academy Eindhoven (the Netherlands), and advised the Dutch government on cultural policy and other public issues. He holds a PhD (University of London) in the politics and sociology of technology. Currently he is developing projects on sustainist culture, under the banner Sustainism Lab.

Earlier books by Michiel Schwarz include *The Technological Culture* (with Rein Jansma, 1989), *Divided We Stand: Redefining Technology, Politics and Social Choice* (with Michael Thompson, 1990) and *Speed: Visions of an Accelerated Age* (with Jeremy Millar, 1998).

⊜ MICHIELSCHWARZ@SUSTAINISM.COM
⊜ SUSTAINISM.COM

DIANA KRABBENDAM

Diana Krabbendam is the co-founder and director of The Beach, a network of creative innovators that is based in Amsterdam. As her career as a designer evolved, she became interested in how design can help to solve complex societal issues, leading her to focus her work on what she terms "creative innovation." Over the last decade, she has been working as a designer, editor and cultural entrepreneur in the field of creative innovation. She recently set up a social innovation hub in the Nieuw-West area of the city of Amsterdam, which she developed to engage the local community in designing their own living environments together with professional designers.

She has a background in graphic design and architecture (graduate Utrecht School of the Arts) and has worked professionally as a designer and creative director for commercial and non-profit clients. She worked as international design director at Randstad and she was editor-in-chief at Dutch design magazine *Items*.

⊜ DIANA@THEBEACH.NU

THE BEACH

The Beach is an Amsterdam-based network of social designers. The Beach initiates and produces projects that are geared at building a more social and sustainable society in collaboration with creative partners, companies, and institutions. Co-design, design of social dialogues, creating new coalitions, and shaping new social meanings is at the core of its practice. Through festivals, conferences, workshops, publications, as well as online platforms, The Beach actively encourages conversations about how design can be a force in social change, locally and beyond.

⊜ THEBEACH.NU

Acknowledgements

Collaboration has been a much used word in this guide. And it was instrumental in making this book what it is: developing this publication was a collaborative effort in many ways. First and foremost, we wish to thank Bas Ruyssenaars, Mira de Graaf, Steffie Verstappen, and Robin Uleman. They formed the core editorial team at The Beach with whom we developed the sustainist design project from start to finish. Their contributions were essential in crafting this guide.

We wish to acknowledge the organisations and people who are behind the twelve design cases that make up the central part of this guide, in particular those who have actively contributed to our project. We thank FairPhone, Bas van Abel and Tessa Wernink; Mine Kafon, Massoud Hassani; WASH United, Thorsten Kiefer and Rima Hanano; Outside Brewery, Henriëtte Waal; Agrocité / Atelier d'Architecture Autogérée, Doina Petrescu and Constantin Petcou; Lamon Luther, Russell Shaw; Rural Spark, Marcel van Heist, Harmen van Heist and Evan Mertens; We Are Here, Jo van der Spek and Joost Pothast; Luchtsingel / ZUS, Elma van Boxel and Kristian Koreman; Global Village Construction Set; Foldit, Seth Cooper; Pig Chase / Utrecht School of the Arts, Clemens Driessen, Evelyn Grooten, Marinka Copier and Irene van Peer.

We would like to say thank you to all who supported our sustainist design project and who contributed to developing the *Sustainist Design Guide*. In particular Danielle Arets,

S. Balaram, Joost Beunderman, Tim Brown, Samantha Castano, Leon Cruickshank, Egbert Fransen, Alastair Fuad-Luke, Meera Goradia, Maarten Hajer, Twan Hofman, Luc Hombergen, Mylene Jonker, Riemer Knoop, Klaas Kuitenbrouwer, Kitty Leering, Madeleine van Lennep, Brigitte van Mechelen, Shashank Mehta, Gayatri Menon, Francesca Miazzo, Bert Mulder, Ino Paap, Amanda Pinatih, Arjan Postma, Marjetica Potrč, Barbara Ruyssenaars, Jörgen van der Sloot, Wina Smeenk, Debra Solomon, Floor van Spaendonck, Anne van Strien, Ekim Tan, Jan van Tiel, Sacha van Tongeren, Fulco Treffers, Raffaella Vandermühlen, Willem Velthoven, Annelys de Vet, Ingrid van der Wacht, Dee Williams, and Evert Ypma. Last but not least, we wish to thank our respective partners, Rody Luton and Frank Blom.

Additionally, we wish to thank all who have made contributions to the opensustainistdesign.net web platform and those who have contributed via Facebook, LinkedIn, and other social media. And we thank the developers of our online platform at Mediamatic.

A special word of thanks goes to Joost Elffers— the co-creator of the *Sustainism manifesto*, which is where it all began—for his inspiration and ideas as we continue to develop sustainism as a cultural perspective. Special thanks also go to Jogi Panghaal who, together with Michiel Schwarz, conducted sustainist design workshops with students at a number of design schools in India.

These very much furthered our thinking.

We owe thanks to Yu-lan van Alphen of the DOEN Foundation for her encouragement and her supportive contributions in the development of the project.

During the past few years we, as well as the members of our editorial team, have shared and exchanged our developing views on sustainist design on different occasions. We have benefitted tremendously from these encounters and they have greatly influenced the direction of our thinking and the content of this guide. We wish to thank the organisers of our workshops, seminars and lectures at the Design Academy Eindhoven / Crisp (in collaboration with Premsela and Capital D), the Utrecht School of the Arts, the Amsterdam Sandberg Institute, Premsela, the PICNIC Festival 2012, Virtueel Platform / HOT100 at PICNIC 2012, Hallo Etsy 2011 (Berlin), the BMW Guggenheim Lab 2011(New York), the D.J. Academy of Design (Coimbatore), the National Design Institute (Ahmedabad & Gandhinagar), and the Srishti School of Art, Design and Technology (Bangalore). We would also like to acknowledge a number of supportive organisations: FreedomLab, Pakhuis de Zwijger, PROUD Europe, Dutch Design Week / Capital D, and What Design Can Do.

Michiel Schwarz
& Diana Krabbendam

Credits

AUTHORS
Michiel Schwarz
Diana Krabbendam
Contributions by
Bas Ruyssenaars
Mira de Graaf
Steffie Verstappen

**EDITORIAL CONCEPT
DEVELOPMENT**
Michiel Schwarz
Diana Krabbendam
Bas Ruyssenaars
Mira de Graaf
Steffie Verstappen
Robin Uleman

TEXT EDITING
Steffie Verstappen

PROOFREADING
Kate Moeller

IMAGE EDITING
Robin Uleman

**PROJECT IDENTITY
& EDITORIAL DESIGN**
Robin Uleman
in dialogue with
Sandra Rabenou

LITHOGRAPHY
Colour & Books

PRINTING
IPP Printers

ISBN
978-90-6369-283-4

Second printing 2014

COPYRIGHT
© 2013
Michiel Schwarz
Diana Krabbendam
The Beach
BIS Publishers

**TEXT COPYRIGHT
CREATIVE COMMONS
2013 BY NC ND**
Michiel Schwarz
Diana Krabbendam

**PHOTOGRAPHS
COPYRIGHT**
© 2013
The photographers

PUBLISHER
BIS Publishers
Het Sieraad
Postjesweg 1
1057 DT Amsterdam
The Netherlands
T +31 (0)20 515 02 30
F +31 (0)20 515 02 39
bis@bispublishers.nl
bispublishers.nl

FUNDING & SUPPORT
We gratefully acknowledge
the financial support that
we received from the
DOEN Foundation and
the Mondriaan Fund for
the development of this
publication. The Beach
acknowledges the support
it receives from the City
of Amsterdam's Arts
& Culture Programme
2013-2016.

YOUR
NOTES
—

And share your ideas at
opensustainistdesign.net